D0507546

Digital Photography: Pictures of Tomorrow

John Larish

Micro Publishing Press
Torrance, California

Digital Photography: Pictures of Tomorrow
John Larish

Published by:
Micro Publishing Press
21150 Hawthorne Blvd., Suite 104
Torrance, CA 90503
(310) 371-5787

First Printing, April, 1992

Printed in the United States of America

ISBN 0-941845-08-7

#25858346

This book is designed to provide information about digital photography. Every effort has been made to make this book as complete and accurate as possible. But no warranty of suitability, purpose, or fitness is implied. The information is provided on an "as-is" basis. The publisher shall have neither liability nor responsibility to any person or entity with respect to any loss or damages in connection with or arising from the information contained in this book.

Many of the designations used by manufacturers and sellers to distinguish their products are claimed as trademarks. Where these designations appear in the book and the authors were aware of a trademark claim, the designations have been printed with initial capital letters—for example PostScript.

PostScript and Adobe are registered trademarks of Adobe Systems, Inc.
Separator, Streamline, Photoshop, and Illustrator are trademarks of Adobe Systems, Inc.
Macintosh, LaserWriter, and AppleTalk are registered trademarks of Apple Computer Inc.
IBM and IBM PC are registered trademarks of IBM Corp.
Aldus, PageMaker, and Aldus FreeHand are registered trademarks of Aldus Corp.
Pantone and PMS are registered trademarks of Pantone Inc.
Mavica is a trademark of Sony Corporation of America
Xapshot is a trademark of Canon USA
All other company and product names are trademarks or registered trademarks of their respective owners.

This book was imaged and printed at Digital Image, Inc., San Diego, CA.

CONTENTS

FOREWORD

A quiet revolution has taken place in the last decade. The century-long use of silver in photography is being supplemented by exciting new digital photography techniques. Some observers feel the quiet revolution is gaining enough momentum to seriously threaten the future of conventional photography.

Traditional silver-based photography users will be familiar with some of the new system elements since they are essentially the same as the old system elements. Things like lenses, F-stops, shutter speeds, depth-of-field, and ASA ratings are all media independent. However, the digital media present a whole new set of challenges to the uninitiated. What happens when the image is captured? How is it processed, stored, reproduced, modified, distributed, and used? What new lessons must be learned? What new opportunities unfold?

John Larish has been a traditional photographic practitioner for several decades and has been involved in digital photography from its beginnings. As a user, writer, publisher, consultant, and developer, he has gained a unique insight into digital photography.

This, his second book on the subject, "puts it all together" for the neophyte and the expert. There is no other single source today for the depth and breadth of the coverage given in this book. This book is exceptional in helping the reader understand the elements of digital photography, the present state-of-the-art, the challenges, difficulties, applications, and future directions.

The book reflects John's extensive practical experience in

the field, and is an indispensable reference for anyone who needs to know what's happening now, and what will probably happen in the future.

Carl Machover
President
Machover Associates Corp.

INTRODUCTION

Today's society is an information society. We saw its beginnings in 1956 when, for the first time in American history, white-collar workers outnumbered blue-collar workers.

We are also in the beginning stage of a new era—the era of digital photography. With the advent of desktop color publishing, multimedia, and digital television, digital photography has become important and essential.

There are many reasons why digital photo images are needed. These include the need to transmit color pictures rapidly from one location to another, the need for image enhancement, and the desire to be able to merge several images to create a new one. New hardware and software for digital imaging have opened up new directions in graphic design. The advent of new color printers and copiers for digital imaging has made hardcopy reproduction of digital photographs easy.

In this book, I identify the key ingredients needed for digital photography. There are numerous applications discussed. There is also a look at the future and where the electronic imaging process is going. I have tried wherever possible to create a generic resource by describing how the various components of a digital photography system work.

Since the announcement of the Sony Mavica electronic still-video camera in 1981, each year has brought us exciting new developments. In a field that moves as dynamically as digital photography, being absolutely up to date is almost impossible. However, it is my hope that this book will give you a good grounding in the essentials of digital photography.

ACKNOWLEDGMENTS

Many people contributed to this book knowingly or un-knowingly. Representatives of organizations such as Eastman Kodak, Sony, Fuji Film, Dicomed—to name a few—all contributed useful information that is included in this book.

To my hard-working wife, Rose Ellen, who put all these words on paper and proofread them, my thanks and my love.

Don Franz, my co-publisher of *Electronic Photography News,* offered helpful advice and encouragement—it was much appreciated.

Special thanks goes to David Pope, whose careful editing added greatly to the finished book and to Jim Frisch, who added his working and practical knowledge to the elements of digital photography.

John Larish
March, 1992

CHAPTER 1

The Basics of Digital Photography

The personal computer has made digital word processing an everyday practice in offices, schools, and homes. Creation and manipulation of digital images on personal computers was made possible by the introduction of graphics and desktop publishing software. The digital photograph is only now coming into wide use, and in the next decade, digital photography can be expected to undergo dynamic growth.

Many people are not aware that film photography and conventional video are analog processes. Analog is a technical term that means the elements vary continuously, with no jumps or steps between them. The image on a silver-halide film or paper, for example, can have a continuous variation from dark to light. The signals that create images on the television screen also are analog.

When an image or anything else is digitized, the continuously varying analog input is converted into discrete, unconnected steps. If the digitizing uses the binary form, the analog signal is converted into a series of on and off signals, usually referred to as 0 and 1. The 0 and 1 cannot be subdivided into 1/2 or any other fraction.

Digitizing an analog signal is done by sampling it at regular intervals. Shorter time intervals generate more accurate sampling. Digitizing an analog signal converts the continuously varying elements into a series of 0s and 1s. Each of the 0s and 1s are stored as individual bits on a computer.

A string, or group, of eight bits is called a byte. A thousand bytes is called a kilobyte, and a million bytes is a megabyte. Kilobyte and megabyte are terms that you will run into over and over again when reading about digital photography and computers.

Japanese Newspapers Overcome Time Difference

APPLICATION BRIEF

The problem was how to get photos of George Bush's inauguration from the U.S. to Japan in time for the morning newspapers, in spite of the 14-hour time difference between Japan and Washington, D.C. The answer was the Sony Still Image Transceiver. After the inauguration ceremonies were completed at 12:45 p.m., the electronic pictures were reviewed and transmitted. Images took five minutes each to transmit.

What is Digital Photography?

In digital photography, the analog shape of an image is converted into digital values. The digitizing can be done inside a digital camera, or it can be done by an external analog-to-digital converter. When an image is digitized, it becomes a series of points. These individual points are called picture elements, or pixels. On the computer screen, each pixel is shown as a tiny square point filled with a degree of color or shade of gray.

One advantage of the digital photograph is that it can be

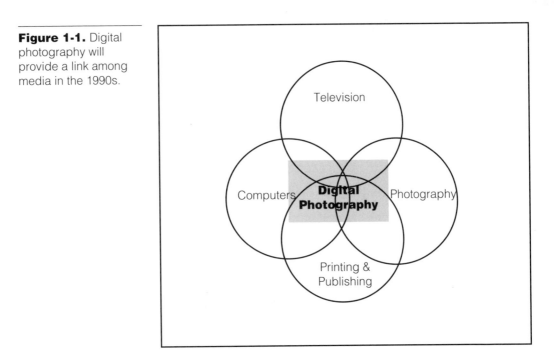

Figure 1-1. Digital photography will provide a link among media in the 1990s.

copied electronically without loss of image quality. Another is that a digital photograph can be enhanced or otherwise modified to improve it. Even the colors in it can be altered.

Digital photography is being increasingly utilized by the mass media. It wasn't long ago that photography, television, printing and publishing, and computers operated as islands, each with its own way of doing things. Film and photographs provided a major means of transferring data and images among the media islands.

Today the digital photograph has given the mass media common form of communication (Figure 1-1). The digital image is easily transmitted and can be used immediately by the recipient. This is not to say that there is still not a need for better interconnectivity or that all the barriers between the various media have been eliminated.

Digital photography is also at the heart of desktop publishing and multimedia. Both create their end products by using pictures and words in digital form. Desktop publishing has already revolutionized the printing industry. Multimedia—the combining of digital photographs, video, sound, and text—promises to become one of tomorrow's most exciting developments (see Chapter Six).

The Digital Photograph Equation

Digital photography is still a mystery to many people. To help with the understanding of the digital photograph, let's begin by defining the digital photograph equation.

The digital photograph equation defines the components of a digital photography system. As in film photography, a camera by itself is not enough. You need the means to process and view the image after it has been captured by the camera. In conventional photography, the film is developed and the image appears as a positive transparency or as a negative that is used to make photographic prints.

In digital photography, a camera is not the only image input device. The image can come from not only digital and analog still-video cameras, but also from video cameras, camcorders, and scanners that are used to digitize images on film or paper.

Digital photography is more than just taking a picture with an electronic camera. The digital photographer, like the traditional film photographer, also needs equipment to develop and enlarge and print the pictures after they are shot with the camera. The digital photographer's darkroom is a computer system. His enlarger is the image processing software he uses on the computer. His negatives and positive prints are the images he brings to his computer screen. His prints come out of color printers, film recorders, or imagesetters.

There are actually only five components in the digital photo equation: *input, processing platform and software, display, storage, and hardcopy output.* For each of the five components, however, there are several types of equipment to choose from (Figure 1-2). Choosing the best equipment for your needs can be complicated, but what usually creates the greatest frustration is setting up the links between the devices.

Figure 1-2. The electronic photograph equation and the types of equipment that are used in each of its five components.

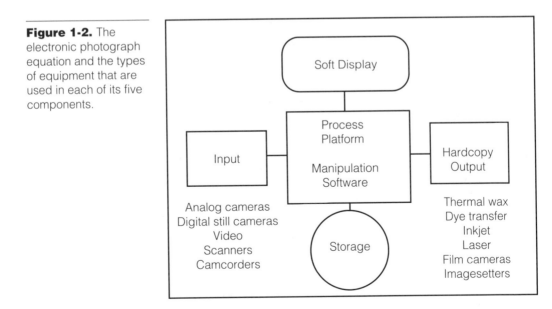

The solution to the interconnectivity problem is the creation of standards that all equipment manufacturers would adhere to. Standards are evolving for almost every portion of the digital photography equation. In some cases, there are multiple standards, which creates additional interconnectivity concerns.

There is the possibility that a standard used in one area is not accepted in a different area. An example of this would be the SCSI input for Apple Macintosh computers, which is not available in PC computers without a special board that allows a SCSI input. This means that you must look carefully at each piece of equipment to be sure that it has the connectivity you desire.

First, let's look at each part of the equation. There are really no big surprises in the components. The digital photograph equation, like a chemical equation, needs to be balanced. For instance, if input is low resolution, then there really is no need for high resolution equipment in the other parts of the equation. The quality of the image will be limited by its original low resolution. On the other hand, if high-resolution input is used, image quality will be lost if the processing platform and hardcopy output equipment cannot handle high-resolution color.

The technology in each component area has been develop-

Electronic Hair Restoring

APPLICATION BRIEF

The Bosley Medical Group in California uses a still video image to show men with thinning hair how they might look with their hair restored. Using a paint system on a computer, the Bosley Group electronically restores the hairline on a copy of the still-video picture, and then shows the customer both the before and after pictures.

ing at a rapid rate. There has been a steady increase in quality and performance while prices, in almost all cases, have been dropped dramatically.

Input

There are several ways of creating digital photographs. The input of these photographs can come from digital or still-video cameras, video cameras, camcorders, or from existing transparency or negative films and prints that can be digitized by a scanner (see Chapter Two).

The advantage of the still-video or digital camera is the instant capture and availability of an image. What makes these cameras useful is that they greatly resemble the conventional film cameras that have been used for years. There is no long learning curve involved in using the new still-video or digital cameras.

With the latest versions of the digital cameras, the images are ready immediately for use in computers for display and printing. In addition, in most cases, the images can be displayed on standard TV sets.

Multimedia offers another dramatic application for these instant digital images.

Electronic images can come also from video cameras or camcorders. While the quality of today's video images is limited by the low resolution currently used for broadcast television, the promise of high-definition television (see Chapter Seven) may offer an alternative means for creating higher quality digital photographs from television.

Film transparencies, negatives, and prints are another vast source for digital photographs. Originally, the only way of digitizing these images was the rotary drum scanner, which still offers the highest quality approach for the conversion of images from films or prints. When you see these beautifully engineered devices, you first think of a high-quality lathe because of the precise rotating drum.

Less expensive than the drum scanners are scanners that use charge-coupled devices (CCDs). Today, flatbed CCD scanners are available for prints and films, as well as special CCD scanners that are sold for digitizing 35mm color slides and negatives.

CCD sensors are limited in their dynamic range for recording color. Their dynamic range is limited by a combination of electronic noise and the size of the collecting area of the

Electronic Photographs Help Find Missing Children

APPLICATION BRIEF

The National Center for Missing and Exploited Children uses electronic photography to help find missing children. PhotoSketch software developed by QMA Corp. of Reston, VA, allows the Center to "age" a child's photograph to show how the child would look years after the photograph had been taken. The software can add 5, 10, or, in at least one case, 30 years. Several children have been found using the aging technique. Photographs of the child, parents, and older siblings are scanned. Once the images are digitized, the child's face is merged with matching parts from the other photographs.

CHILD AT AGE 1 WHEN ABDUCTED   AGE PROGRESSION AS 9 YEAR OLD   RECOVERY PHOTOGRAPH AT AGE 9

CCD sensor. CCDs in video cameras and camcorders can pick up only eight bits per color pixel, which produces only 256 shades of colors. Drum scanners can pick up from 8 to 14 bits per pixel. For full color processing on personal computers, usually 24 bits per pixel are used. This will produce 16,700,000 colors (Figure 1-3).

Processing Platforms and Software

There are three major platforms used today for digital photography—the Apple Macintosh, PCs (IBM or compatibles), and Unix-based machines such as the Sun workstation. Many boards have been created for both Macintosh

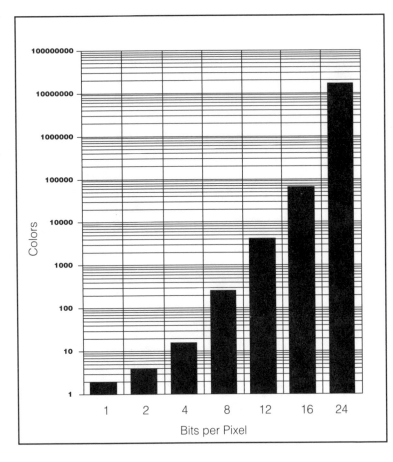

Figure 1-3. In a computer system, the number of colors that can be displayed or printed out depends on the number of bits per pixel used. Eight bits per pixel allows the display of 256 different colors, while 24 bits per pixel allows over 16.7 million.

and PC platforms that allow the conversion of analog images from video systems to be converted into a digital form.

Storage on the systems has been a problem because of the large file size of color digital images. While a video image may take only a half megabyte of memory, a high-resolution scanned image may require 250 megabytes or more of memory. The RAM requirements for image processing also are high.

In the mid-1980s, the Macintosh personal computer along with Adobe System's PostScript and Aldus' PageMaker created what came to be called desktop publishing. In the late 1980s, image enhancement software was developed for scanning images and modifying the scanned images.

Microsoft's Windows provided a graphical user interface for the PC computers. A variety of software packages offer digital image enhancement and typesetting functions on the PC platform. New software packages for color desktop publishing are also beginning to appear, which is further increasing the need for digital photographs.

Unix-based workstations using specially developed software packages have also proved to be popular for image manipulation. What has made these platforms attractive is their capability for multimedia as well as their speed of processing.

Faster Drivers Licenses

APPLICATION BRIEF

Future drivers license kiosks in California will not only administer eye tests, but will also take electronic photographs. Some see this as a way of completely eliminating the trip to the motor vehicle bureau altogether.

Displays

On the Macintosh platform, there are several choices for displaying color images. Many users are satisfied with the color monitor sold by Apple for the Macintosh. Others find that they need screens with higher resolution or larger color displays. These can be purchased from third-party vendors such as E-Machines and Radius, which offer full-page and two-page displays. Other developers offer accelerator and graphic boards for the Mac.

Most of the PC color display systems available today use the VGA mode or the equivalent, which has far less resolution than a digital photograph. There are, however, a number of graphic boards for PCs that can produce Super VGA resolution of more than 1000 by 1000 pixels on CRT color displays (see Chapters Three and Five).

LCD screens, both color and black-and-white, have been at the VGA level. Until such time as monitors are developed for high definition television (HDTV), there will be a limit on the resolution of the LCD monitors available for computer systems.

While plasma screens have been demonstrated, both in monochrome and in color, it appears that it will be some time before production screens of this type are available.

Electronic Still-Photo Dentistry

◆

**APPLICATION
BRIEF**

The Oral Scan Computer Imaging System from Lester A. Dine Inc. uses a special video camera to capture still images of teeth. These images can be enhanced to show the potential effects of restoration work. A Polaroid Freeze Frame Recorder is used to produce a photographic print.

Storage

Color digital images take up large amounts of memory when they are stored. The old proverb that a picture is worth a thousand words doesn't even begin to come close to the size of the stored digital photograph. Even the simplest digital image may be the equal of 500 pages of text, and a high-resolution image may require some five hundred times more memory (see Chapter Two).

Magnetic disk storage is attractive in terms of cost per megabyte. Both fixed and removable Winchester drives that can store hundreds of megabytes are available. One drawback is the relatively slow speed of data transfer, which can impede the handling of large image files.

Optical media have proved to be particularly advantageous for the storage of digital photographs. Optical media includes write-once read-many (WORM) disks and tapes, erasable optical disks, and optical memory cards. A number of CD-ROM disk drives are available for personal computers.

Until recently, the main drawback to erasable optical media has been a limitation on the speed at which they are able to write and then read the information stored. Improvements to the optical erasable material have been made and the write/read speed now begins to approach that of Winchester drives.

New technology such as the Kodak Photo CD will allow high-quality color photo images to be stored in non-erasable memory for archival purposes with retrieval available from a Photo CD, CD-I, or CD-ROM-XA player.

With the availability of larger and lower-cost RAM chips

solid-state memory becomes practical for storage of single images. Solid-state memory provides a distinct speed advantage for processing images.

Environment Benefits from Electronic Photography

◆

APPLICATION BRIEF

At Northrop Corp., the adoption of the Sony Electronic Photography System has eliminated the use of 1.2 million gallons of water in processing photos as well as the electrical energy required to heat the water to 90 degrees. Additionally, more than 5000 gallons of hazardous waste per year has been eliminated. The expected savings are more than $4.3 million over the next five years.

Hard Copy

A few years ago, thermal wax printers were the only option for printing digital color images and the results were not even close to photographic quality. Today, the quality of thermal wax printers has improved sufficiently to allow them to be used for proofing purposes for digital color photographs.

For higher quality printing of digital photographs, there are several excellent choices. Thermal dye transfer, inkjet, and other printers that use silver-halide photographic paper produce digital images with photo-like qualities, both from the standpoint of resolution and color saturation. Color copiers are also being used to print digital images, and the quality of their output is suitable for many commercial applications (see Chapter Five).

Film "originals" can be produced by a number of different film recorders. These devices can output digital images on either color negative or transparency film with resolutions from 2000 to 16,000 lines. Imagesetters can also produce either color transparencies and color negatives, as well as color separations for printing.

Finally, there are now computer-to-plate and computer-to-press systems that are suitable for reproducing thousands of copies. These systems move the digital images directly from the computer to a printing press.

Understanding Color and Standards

Color is color, at least to the eyes of many people. However, computers and the printing press create colors in entirely different ways. Computers use an additive system, combining red, green, and blue light to create colors. The printing press uses a subtractive system, using cyan, yellow, and magenta dyes to absorb (subtract) certain colors in the white light that strikes the page.

Television sets and computer screens utilize red, green, and blue (RGB) phosphors. All the other colors that we see on the screen are created by mixing these three colors. Can we create all possible colors using just 24 bits per pixel? It's very unlikely even in the best of monitors since we are limited by the output of the phosphors used in the CRTs. In most printing systems and color copiers, CYMK (cyan, yellow, and magenta plus black) is used.

The human eye responds more to changes in lighter colors than to changes in the more saturated colors. This lack of uniformity in what is perceived in color space presents a problem to those who want to be able to measure color differences.

In 1931 the CIE (Commission International de l'Eclairage) created the first color standard for international use. It was based on measurements of visual conditions, but it lacked visual uniformity. In 1976, the CIE-LUV color metrics were developed, which achieves a greater correlation between mathematical distances between colors and the visual differences. Several companies are adapting the CIE-LUV standard to desktop publishing.

Part of the problem that digital photography faces is that the printing, photographic, and computer industries each have different standards for color and ways of dealing with color. Some of the standards are based on the way things have been done in that particular industry, and in some cases because of the physical equipment used, as well as the research and development, of that particular industry.

Printers use the subtractive process—CYMK works very well for printing on a white surface. In the printing process, black is used to create saturated colors.

For the photographic industry, CYM dyes are used to create color images both in films and in reflection prints.

The computer industry CRT displays use red, green, and blue, which are added to the black surface of the CRT.

The different color systems are a problem. Ideally, a new color standard should be developed to replace all previous standards so that we have a fresh start for digital photography, desktop publishing, and multimedia. While this is idealistic, it is not realistic, and more important, it would be prohibitively expensive to discard the standards that are in use today.

Even the simple matter of how many bits of color are needed for creating a complete spectrum of colors on a computer will bring an argument because of the limitations of the display screen. Most CRT screens are unable to reproduce the full spectrum of colors, but there is the need for that full spectrum of colors for making color prints or transparencies.

While much has been accomplished in the development of standards to make all the pieces of the digital photograph equation fit together, there are still multiple formats and multiple standards that affect each connecting point of the digital photograph equation. That means that you must look at each part of the digital photograph equation, and make sure that you know what output and input you need so that you can mix-and-match equipment to do the job.

Figure C2-13. An image created using a Sony two-chip ProMavica camera. (Courtesy Sony Corporation of America)

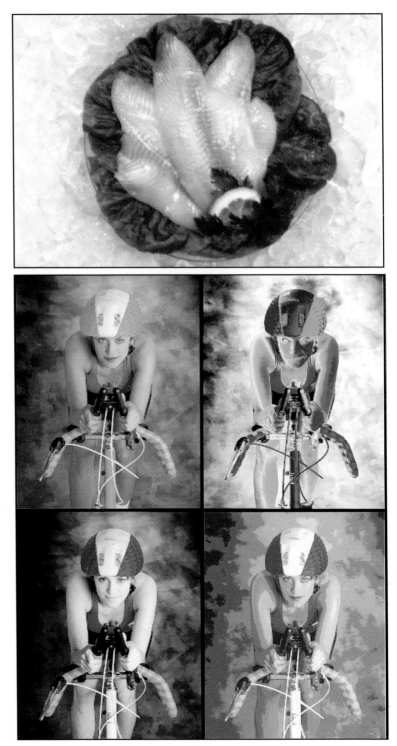

Figure C3-10. Examples of how color photo retouching systems can modify an image. In upper-left image, the helmet color, shirt, logo on bike, and lock of hair have been altered. Other examples demonstrate solarization, posterization, and desaturation (black-and-white conversion). (Courtesy Dicomed)

Figure C3-11.
Program cover produced using Networked Picture Systems' color image-editing system. (Courtesy Networked Picture Systems)

Figure C3-12.
Example of how a color compression system can reduce file size without serious degradation to image quality. (Courtesy Telephoto Communications Inc.)

Figure C5-7. An example of image quality produced by the Kodak XL7700 continuous-tone, thermal-dye transfer printer. (Courtesy Eastman Kodak)

Rodeo Coverage With Digital Photography

**APPLICATION
BRIEF**

Magazine photographer Shelly Katz took this photo of the steer wrestling event at the Mesquite Championship Rodeo in Mesquite, TX. Katz used the Kodak Digital Camera System to shoot the photograph, which was output on the Kodak XL7700 printer.

Figure C6-8. An example of Iterated Systems' fractal compression. The original image (left) required 768 kilobytes of storage; the compressed image (right) required only 10.5 kilobytes. (Courtesy Iterated Systems Inc.)

CHAPTER 2

Creating Digital Photographs

There are many ways of creating digital photographs. They can be generated by direct electronic capture of the image by a digital camera, or by converting an analog image captured by a camcorder or still-video camera. If you have photographic images that exist as prints, negatives, or transparencies, you can digitize them using one of several types of scanners.

When someone asks what is the best way to capture an image, it is almost necessary to give an "it all depends" answer. First of all, it depends on what you are looking for as the final result. If you are looking for glossy magazine quality, then a very expensive rotary-drum scanner will probably be the only device that will meet your needs. In the mid-cost range (between $1000 and $20,000), there are many ways for capturing images, and these mid-range devices will more than adequately meet the needs of most users.

In this chapter, we will start by looking at the various forms of electronic still cameras, both analog and digital. From there, we will go to video systems, and finally to the multitude of scanners that are available. We will also be looking at systems for electronically storing your digital photographs.

Electronic Image-Capture Devices

What made today's camcorders, still-video cameras, and flatbed scanners possible was the development of electronic image-capture devices. First there were image tubes for TV cameras and remote sensing applications. In the 1970s, the charged-coupled device (CCD) appeared and eventually replaced most of the image tubes, except for a few specialized applications. Image tubes are still found in applications where low-light imaging and light intensification is needed. CCD devices cannot, in most cases, amplify light.

Image Tubes

Until the late 1970s, image tubes dominated the market for video cameras, image sensing, industrial applications, and other applications in which the capture of video images was needed.

The Vidicon camera tube utilizes an electron beam to scan a light-sensitive, photoconductive target (Figure 2-1). A transparent conductor layer applied to the front side of the photoconductor serves as the signal or target electrode. In operation, an electron beam charges the back side of the target. When a light pattern is focused on the photoconductor, the conductivity increases in the illuminated areas and the back side of the target charges to more

Figure 2-1. Basic elements of a television image tube.

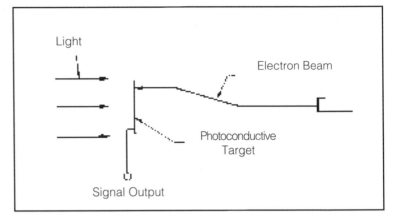

positive values. The electron beam deposits electrons on the positively coated areas, which creates a capacitively-coupled signal at the signal electrode.

Vidicon tubes, especially some found in military surveillance applications, can be of superior quality to solid-state devices that are currently available. A general problem with tubes is that, if they are not handled carefully, stray debris from within the tube may fall on the charged surface and produce permanent artifacts that cannot be removed, and this will cause a loss of information.

Charge-Coupled Devices

Invented in the late 1960s by researchers at Bell Laboratories, the charge-coupled device (CCD) was initially intended to be a new type of computer memory circuit. It soon became apparent that the CCD had many other potential applications, including signal processing and imaging—the latter because of its sensitivity to light. The CCD's early promise as a memory device has since disappeared, but its superb ability to handle light has made it a critical part of today's image-sensing devices.

Figure 2-2. A Kodak CCD sensor. (Courtesy Eastman Kodak Company)

CCDs are simple devices that generate packets of electrons that represent, in analog form, the degree of illumination. The CCD is efficient throughout the visible light spectrum and can respond to very low levels of light (Figure 2-2).

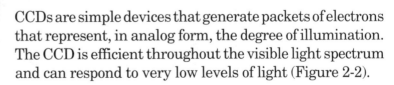

Space-Age Photography From the Space Shuttle

APPLICATION BRIEF

As part of the Johnson Space Center's Electronic Still Camera project, shuttle astronauts tried out a NASA-developed digital still camera. They transmitted the digital monochrome photographs to earth in real time. Technicians had hard copy images within one hour.

On the shuttle, digital images are stored on removable hard disks or small optical disks. The images are compressed and transmitted as a digital stream to a ground satellite in New Mexico, which sends the images via satellite to the Johnson Space Center.

Using a Truevision TARGA+64 videographics board and ImageScale Plus software from Electronic Imagery, astronauts can improve the resolution of images before transmission.

There are two basic forms of CCDs. Area arrays are a rectangular array of horizontal and vertical pixels, while linear arrays are a single row of pixels. Area-array CCDs have found their way into applications such as periscopes in submarines, video cameras, scientific satellites, and astronomical telescopes. Linear CCD arrays are found in photocopiers, facsimile machines, and even in the local supermarket bar-code readers at the cash registers.

Linear arrays have been especially popular because of their high resolution and low cost. Today it is possible to obtain linear CCD arrays with 5000 to 8000 pixels in a single array. How much further this technology will go is only a matter of design and silicon capability.

The area-array CCD has already reached a level of 4096 by 4096 pixels and even this capability is being expanded. In the foreseeable future, it should be possible to have arrays of four times that amount.

CCD imagers operate in a series of four steps. First, the light reaching it is converted into proportional quantities of electrons. These packets of electrons are stored in a capacitor. To retrieve the information held by electron packets, they are transferred to a read-out stage and finally converted into an analog voltage signal. For proper operation, the sensor must have darkness for the transfer function.

Color is achieved with CCDs in two ways. For more sophisticated approaches, where greater color information and sharpness are desired, three different sensors are used. Light coming through the camera lens is separated with prisms into three separate colors, red, green, and blue (RGB) and each color is read by a different CCD. The signals from the three CCDs are either combined as a video color signal or made available as separate RGB signals.

The other method of obtaining color information is through

the use of color filters on the face of the sensor. With most CCD sensors, these color filters are one unit of a red filter, one of a blue filter, and one, two or three units of green filters. This increase in green produces greater sharpness and a more linear color but will sometimes produce some artifacts such as moire patterns.

If a single pixel has more light than it is capable of recording, the overexposure travels along with the other information and causes a streaking or blooming. Some recent CCDs have been developed with anti-blooming protection.

There are some other forms of solid-state image sensors available. In rotary drum scanners, photodiodes are used because they have a spectral response similar to that of the human eye and produce a higher bit rate for each color scan.

Charge-injection devices (CIDs) also are used as imagers. Unlike CCDs, CIDs do not use a charge movement for readout. The charge in a CID remains stationary and selective readout is made of individual pixels. Because of this, CIDs are particularly good at resisting smearing or blooming.

Some of the considerations in evaluating a sensor for functions such as digital photography include the sensitivity of the sensor as it relates to noise. Noise is located at the low end of the dynamic range. This is particularly important when there are low levels of light where noise may become very substantial.

There are three types of noise to be considered: dark current noise, which is the result of a thermal generation (heat) and most specifications for sensors include information on dark noise; fixed pattern noise, which is repeated from frame to frame; and temporal or time variant noise, caused by the integrated circuits used with the sensor.

Even more important in considering a sensor is the dynamic range of the sensor. This is the useful signal output of the sensor and will greatly affect the number of bits per color. If there is a great deal of noise in the sensor, it will be difficult to obtain a very good bit-per-color imaging from a particular sensor.

Consumer camcorders and other video cameras are likely to have area arrays of 380,000 to 390,000 pixels. These area arrays are manufactured by a number of companies. Sensors of much higher quality are manufactured by Eastman Kodak, Loral, Tektronix, and Texas Instruments.

A new generation of sensors with microlenses is beginning to appear. The Sony HyperHAD (Whole Accumulated Diode) has a microlens over the silicon. These tiny elements collect light that would ordinarily fall on non-sensitive areas and concentrate the light on the actual imaging silicon area of the sensor. Sony claims an increased sensitivity of one full f-stop because of the microlens.

Solving Crimes with Digital Photos

APPLICATION BRIEF

The San Jose, CA Police Department has put to work a new system called Forcefield II Law Enforcement Booking and Subject Identification System. The system operates on a DEC Microvax system and uses 12-inch WORM optical disks. Each disk can store up to 300,000 mug shots.

During an investigation, suspects can be sorted by typing characteristics into the system and then pulling from the large database of digitized photos.

Analog Still-Video Photography

Until 1981, when Sony introduced the Mavica still-video camera, making photographs by any process other than silver halide was just a dream in the minds of researchers. Sony's analog still-video system used a 2-inch floppy disk with 52 tracks of information, 50 of which were capable of recording a field of video information or alternatively, a field followed by 9.6 seconds of sound, with two fields joining together to form an entire video frame. The two additional tracks were control tracks necessary for the storage of the analog information recorded on the disk.

The analog signal recorded on the video floppy disk was similar to the form of the recording in color video tape recorders with the exception that the two color-different signals are recorded in line sequence so that horizontal and vertical color detail is matched (Figure 2-3).

Figure 2-3. A TDK VF-1 2-inch video floppy disk. (Courtesy TDK Electronics Corp.)

Color still-video photography offers a better way of capturing images than trying to take them from a videotape. The electronic mechanisms of the still-video camera are designed to freeze an image and synchronize a flash—a challenge for most conventional video cameras or camcorders without special adapters.

An organization called the Electronic Still Camera Standardization Committee (ESCSC) developed the original standard for still-video analog products in 1983. This standard fits the NTSC format we use in our home television.

Later, a hi-band standard was developed that improved the picture quality to a level of 500 lines of resolution from the original 360 lines. The new standard was recorded on the same analog format disk and hi-band playback units were fully compatible for the playback of original-standard recordings, but the hi-band recordings were not capable of playback on standard players.

Although the still-video floppy disk looks similar to the 2-inch floppy disk used in some computers, the format and configuration are different. The video floppy disk consists of a metal-coated disk 1.85 inches in diameter in a sealed plastic case that is 2.4 inches by 2.1 inches by 0.14 inches. The disk spins at 3600 rpm with one field being recorded in one revolution. The capacity of a still-video floppy disk, translated into computer terms, is between 740 kilobytes and 1 megabyte.

Because the still-video system uses a floppy disk, many people think that the system is a digital system—it is not— it's analog! The 2-inch floppy disk is one of the limitations still to be overcome for higher resolution electronic still-video systems.

The resolution capability of the CCD sensor is a basic limitation of still-video cameras and camcorders. Until recently, one of the highest resolution analog still-video sensors was the 600,000-pixel sensor in a Canon still-video camera that is no longer available. Kodak has developed a 1.3 million-pixel CCD for its professional digital camera system.

The first of the original standard electronic still-video cameras also came from Canon. These cameras resembled conventional Canon 35mm cameras and actually used the same lenses interchangeably. When you compare the still-video cameras to 35mm conventional cameras, the major difference was that the focal length of a lens was about four times as long. A 50mm standard lens for a 35mm camera would act like a 200mm lens on the still-video camera. While this may offer benefits to law enforcement agencies for surveillance, where long focal length lenses are used

commonly, for the average photographer it was very difficult to find a short focal-length lens for shooting a normal image.

Cameras that looked much like the "point-and-shoot" 35mm cameras began to appear for electronic still photography. The Canon RC-470 was followed by the Canon Xapshot, both of which are point-and-shoot models (Figures 2-4 and 2-5).

Sony introduced the Sony ProMavica 5000, with two standard CCD chips. One chip was used for luminance and the other chip was used for chroma (color). This camera made it possible to achieve the full horizontal resolution capability of the hi-band standard, something that few other cameras were able to achieve at the time while using the standard 360,000-pixel CCD sensor (Figure 2-6).

Figure 2-5. The Canon XapShot still-video Camera is a Hi-band field recorder and player. (Courtesy Canon USA)

Minolta, which was the first to market an autofocus conventional 35 mm, single-lens reflex cameras, came up with a different approach to electronic still photography. As they designed their Minolta Maxxum™ camera, they included

Figure 2-6. The Sony MVC-5000 still-video camera uses two separate chips for image pickup, one for chroma and one for luminance, to improve picture quality. (Courtesy Sony Corp. of America)

an electronic still-video back that had a supplementary lens. This supplementary lens reduced focal length of the standard lenses by a factor of two, instead of the factor of four encountered by lenses on other electronic still cameras. Thus, a 50mm lens became a 100mm lens and a wide angle 28mm lens closely approximated the standard 50mm lens on the camera. The electronic still back proved to be useful for biomedical photography and other applications where screen images were useful (Figure 2-7).

While a number of manufacturers have shown prototypes of analog still-video cameras, the only companies actively marketing these cameras have been Canon, Sony, Panasonic, and until recently, Minolta.

In the last few years, other cost-effective imaging devices have appeared. New variations and modifications of basic sensors have made them practicable for camera focusing, for white light balancing, and for all of the various functions needed by the complete electronic still-video camera.

Applications for the analog still-video camera have been primarily found in the industrial and commercial areas. The point-and-shoot cameras, with their ability to create instant pictures that can be translated into computer digital images (see Chapter Three), are particularly attractive to a wide range of people because of their low cost.

Figure 2-7. The Minolta still-video Back SB-70 allowed Minolta Maxxum 7000 conventional film cameras to be used for still-video photography also.

Other industrial applications utilizing higher-quality cameras have been in public relations, destructive testing, and scientific and medical areas. One of the largest users of electronic still-video cameras has been the U.S. Government, which uses them for a wide range of surveillance and intelligence applications, including battlefield imaging.

When combined with suitable software programs, analog electronic still-video cameras can be used for publishing. The images produced are ready for electronic prepress. Some use has been made of still-video cameras for creating television commercials. The hi-band cameras meet broadcast resolution requirements and can be useful tools for creating single images or a progression of images for inclusion within commercials.

New still-video cameras are all hi-band cameras. Most manufacturers have chosen to go the route of field recording, which give 50 images per disk, as opposed to frame recording, which give only 25 images per disk. There are some subjects that would be better reproduced if the frame option were available, but the field image is adequate for many applications.

Almost all of the still-video cameras use the 380,000-pixel CCD image sensor, which produces a good quality video image. Lenses for most prototype still-video cameras have been zoom lenses with macro focusing. This, in the future, may offer creative opportunities for the person using the electronic still-video camera.

There is still the problem of the video look of still-video pictures. The film-look that people have become used to with the 35mm film camera has not been achieved by still-video cameras. The inherent contrast of still-video camera images, combined with low exposure indexes, limits the creative use of the still-video camera. Some of the low-light limitations have been overcome by providing f1.2, f1.4 or f1.8 lenses on some of the new prototype cameras. The real answer will be an improvement in the CCD sensors, but this may be a problem since most CCDs are used in the growing market of camcorders and the electronic manufacturers of camcorders are satisfied with the present performance of CCDs.

Both Canon and Sony have made major efforts at promoting analog still-video to consumers with lackluster results. Bringing an image to the video screen involves some cabling hassles that are no problem to the videophile but are major obstacle for the average consumer. The consumer may be able to connect a VCR, but the addition of a still-video camera with its video signal outputs is a challenge in the best of video systems.

Still Video in Broadcasting

APPLICATION BRIEF

Master control for the New Jersey Network, a public television station serving the New York and Philadelphia markets, uses a Sony ProMavica Recorder as a master control system. A still-video recorder with a time-base corrector provides a storage site for graphics using standard 2-inch video floppy disks.

Available Analog Cameras

The first analog still-video cameras to reach the marketplace came from Canon. Sony soon followed with the ProMavica camera. Manufacturers such as Casio, Fuji, and Konica introduced cameras, or backs for cameras, which were later discontinued.

Prototype cameras were shown by companies such as Chinon, Copal, Olympus, Pentax, Sanyo, Vivitar, and Yashica. These prototype cameras showed interesting features, but none of them were brought into production.

Canon continues to supply still-video cameras, but concentrates its marketing to business applications such as insurance, real estate, and other areas where simple point-and-shoot cameras can be used.

Figure 2-8. The Sony Mavica camera can record 9.6 seconds of audio as well as capture field images in Hi-band format. (Courtesy Sony Corp. of America)

Sony has gone in two different directions with their cameras. A point-and-shoot camera (Figure 2-8), which records 9.6 seconds of sound as well as pictures, has found its place in the commercial marketplace. For professionals, there is the Sony dual-chip camera. It can be expected that Sony will eventually move to three-chip still-video cameras.

Figure 2-9. The Canon Xapshot still-video computer imaging kit provides a camera, board, and software for using still-video images in a PC or Macintosh computer. (Courtesy Canon USA)

Panasonic has also adopted the point-and-shoot concept and has directed its marketing to commercial application of still-video cameras.

More interesting is the availability of complete kits, such as Canon's Xapshot kit, that include a camera, processing board, and software designed to take the analog still-video image from the camera and create a digital file for use in Macintosh or PC computers. (Figure 2-9). A 2-inch floppy disk player from Canon can produce an RGB signal that is ready for computer digital input.

Still Photo Saves TV Studio Space

APPLICATION BRIEF

While one system for storage of images takes 25 square feet, WCIU, serving Greater Chicago, Illinois, Milwaukee, Wisconsin, and South Bend, Indiana, uses a Sony ProMavica Player Recorder, which takes a few inches of rack space, as a production system for on-air graphics.

Digital Still Photography

The big advantage of digital video lies in its signal processing capability. Digital processing can eliminate picture artifacts and improve color and sharpness. The stored digital image can be re-recorded without the loss of image quality, which is a distinct advantage for archival storage of images.

Broadcasters are beginning to use digital video systems for electronic news gathering, editing, and other production jobs. Digital tape recorders, as well as production equipment, are available today. The real question to be asked about digital television is not how, but when. We have the technology to do the job today—at least the first versions—but the real driving force will be the industrial, commercial, and educational uses of the multimedia systems that are now appearing in the marketplace. For the home market, digital video technology may be a little more distant.

The various shades and hues of nature that surround us are analog. Conventional video recording is analog. The recording is continuous both in value and in time. A digital signal, on the other hand, contains both value and time as non-continuous numbers.

When a photographic image is captured by a still-video camera, a video camcorder, or a scanner, the first step in these devices is the production of an analog image. The real excitement comes when we take an analog-to-digital converter and change the analog shape of the image to a series of digital values. Once the image is digitized, then we can use the power of the digital computer to do many enhancements or modifications to that image.

An analog waveform is a continuously varying value over time, changing like waves on a body of water. To convert this to a digital signal, both the value and the time must be converted into non-continuous, numeric values. The process of time determination is called sampling, which is done at equal steps of time. The conversion of the value, or amplitude, into discrete values is called quantizing. The combined process is called analog-to-digital conversion (A/D conversion) or digitizing.

This conversion process is an approximation. If the sampling rate is low, the result will be a very inaccurate representation of the signal. If the sampling rate is high, an almost exact copy of the original signal can be achieved. Analog-to-digital conversion chips have been developed that can sample at 300 million samples per second. In the case of color, the red, green, and blue information is handled as three separate sets of data to produce three sets of digital information. Three A/D circuits are used and the encoding is done simultaneously.

As we digitize an image, we create a series of adjacent points called pixels. If the resolution of the display system is low, it will be possible to see the individual pixels. This is called pixelation.

Available Digital Still Cameras and Systems

Digital camera systems are beginning to appear. Most of these systems have the same CCDs found in analog still-video cameras, but the picture information is converted in the camera to a digital signal and stored in either a RAM or ROM memory.

Digital photography cameras have taken two separate directions. There are cameras which still produce a standard NTSC signal for standard television sets. Other digital cameras produce pure digital signals without any reference to the NTSC signal. The resolution offered by the various non-NTSC cameras ranges all the way from very low to very high.

One digital camera began as a joint development by Fuji

Figure 2-10. The Toshiba Model MC200 Digital Still Camera System uses memory cards for recording digital still-video images. (Courtesy Toshiba America Corp.)

Photo Film and Toshiba Corp. Later both companies came out with products that were no longer compatible. The Toshiba digital still-video camera (Figure 2-10) stores 12 images on an 8-megabit memory card, while the Fuji camera stores either five frames in fine mode, 10 frames in normal mode, or 21 frames in economy mode (Figure 2- 11). The Fuji camera uses an image compression chip that the company developed with Zoran Corp. The Fuji camera uses a 1/2-inch, 390,000-pixel CCD, and the Toshiba camera has a 2/3-inch, 400,000-pixel CCD. Two different memory cards are offered by Toshiba and one by Fuji.

At a 1990 German international photo show, Photokina, eight manufacturers showed digital still cameras. In addition to Fuji and Toshiba, who had market-ready systems, Olympus, Ricoh, Chinon, Konica, Minolta, and Kodak showed prototype digital cameras or backs. With the exception of Kodak, all the manufacturers were using memory cards. Their cards closely resembled the memory cards that are used in the laptop computers. The Olympus digital still camera used a compression algorithm that enables it to store 52 images on a 2-megabyte card.

Figure 2-11. The Fuji DS-100 Digital Electronic Camera can record up to 21 frames on an 8 megabit DRAM card. (Courtesy Fuji Photo Film)

It is evident that a standard for digital imaging and the

Figure 2-12. The Kodak Professional Digital Camera System (DCS) provides a means of capturing high-quality digital color or black-and-white images and rapidly transmitting them. (Courtesy Eastman Kodak Company)

associated memory cards is needed. Sixteen Japanese manufacturers met in 1990 to formulate a memory card standard for consumer still-video cameras. Included were Fuji, Nikon, Olympus, Minolta, Asahi Optical, Matsushita, Sony, Hitachi, Toshiba, and Sharp.

One of the smallest digital cameras is the pocket-size Dycam camera that provides a black-and-white 376 by 240-pixel image and the ability to download stored images directly to a PC or Macintosh computer.

Polaroid created a black-and-white CCD still-video camera system called HiRES, which recorded images on standard VHS tape. Polaroid felt that the storage of the large amount of data was most practical on VHS tape and standard VCR decks.

The Kodak Professional Digital Camera System (DCS) blends conventional camera and digital imaging technologies to produce high-quality images. With the system, photographers work with a familiar camera body and lens combination—the Nikon F3 camera (Figure 2-12).

In terms of aperture settings, metering, shutter speeds, and focus mechanism, the digital Nikon F3 camera operates essentially the same as it would with film. The Nikon F3 body requires no special viewfinder optics or modifications. With the DCS, a special interchangeable focusing screen is provided that matches the size of the imaging area.

The imaging area of the DCS is only half that of a 35mm film frame, so the focal lengths of the Nikon-mount lenses are effectively doubled. For example, a conventional 50mm lens becomes a 100mm lens with the system.

The DCS offers a choice of two camera backs, one color, one monochrome, that replace the standard back. The color and monochrome backs contain a Kodak developed 1280 by

1024-pixel CCD imager. The full-frame imager is specifically designed for still photography and has 16-micron pixels for improved light sensitivity.

A camera winder operates at a rate of up to 2.5 captures per second. This winder is equipped with an exposure feedback indicator, flexible cable, and tripod mount.

The Kodak Digital Storage Unit (DSU) stores up to 158 uncompressed images, or 400 to 600 compressed images. The digital storage unit incorporates a 200-megabyte Winchester disk and JPEG-compatible image compression capability.

With the color back, the DCS produces images equivalent to exposure indexes (EI) of 200, 400 (the system's nominal speed), 800, and 1600. The monochrome camera back delivers images equivalent to EI 400, 800 (system nominal speed), 1600, and 3200.

The digital storage unit is equipped with an 8-megabyte dynamic random-access memory (DRAM) buffer capable of storing up to a six-image burst. Since many photographers fire more images per burst, a 32-megabyte buffer capable of storing up to a 24-image burst has been developed as a system option.

Captured images can be immediately reviewed on a 4-inch monochrome LCD monitor that is built into the digital storage unit. Images can be transmitted by modem directly from the digital storage unit to any computer that can accept the ANPA/IPTC file format.

Other approaches have been tried to create a digital camera for use in commercial photography studios. For example, the Tessera system provides a captured image of 2048 by 2048 pixels with CYMK images taking one minute to capture.

Sony digital studio camera system uses three CCDs, one for red, one green, and one blue, with a resolution of 1550 by 575 pixels, and after conversion from analog to digital, an 8-bit per color RGB signal is produced. The Sony system pictures are made instantly with electronic flash (see Color Figure C2-15).

Another approach to digital photography is the Optoscan module, which can be placed in the back of a Rolleiflex 6000 camera. Using a 5000-pixel linear array, an RGB scan takes 90 seconds and produces a 5000 by 5000 pixel image with 8 bits per color. This system can be used for studio catalog work or any application in which motion is not captured.

Superconductor Research and Electronic Still Photography

APPLICATION BRIEF

Researchers at the DuPont Experimental Station are replacing conventional photo records with digital still records of high-magnification electron microscope images for research on new semiconductors and other electronic materials.

Images are captured directly from the microscope using still-video and these images can be reviewed immediately after they have been recorded, enhanced, archived, and printed. Hi-band Sony still-video equipment is used in conjunction with a digital image processor and thermal dye transfer printer for output.

Scanners

The basic function of a scanner is to digitize images. When a scanner digitizes a photograph or other illustration, it converts light reflected from the image—analog information—into digital format. In most cases, CCDs are used to measure the reflected light. In many scanners, the CCDs are arranged in a single line, a linear array. Camera-based scanners and video minicams are more likely to use rectangular, or area, arrays of CCD elements. Some scanners use photodiodes instead of CCDs, but the basic technique is the same.

Rotary-drum scanners are used for very high-resolution digitizing. These scanners use a very fine light beam to scan the image. The reflected (or transmitted) light is captured by photomultipliers and converted into a digital signal.

Image scanning has become popular and a variety of desktop scanners that use linear CCD arrays are available. Recently, full-color scanners with three rows of CCDs, one each for red, green, and blue, have been marketed. This tricolor array allows full-color scanning with a single pass of the scanning head.

The number of elements in the CCD array determines the resolution of the images that are scanned. An 8.5-inch linear array with 2540 elements has 300 elements per inch and can produce a digitized image with a resolution of 300 dots per inch (dpi).

Standard desktop scanners operate in the 300 to 400 dpi range. There are scanners offering resolutions from 1000 to 5000 dpi, but as you reach for higher resolutions, the cost jumps sharply and so does the scan time and file size. Some of the higher resolution scanners can take 10 minutes or more to scan a color image, and the file size can be more than 200 megabytes, not an easily handled data file.

Another consideration in color scanning is the color depth of each scanned red, green, and blue pixel. It takes six bits or more per color to assure a natural looking color.

Once your photographs or illustrations are in a digital format, the images can be electronically manipulated in various ways using off-the-shelf software.

In choosing a scanner, a number of things must be considered. First, what is it that you will be scanning? Artwork and photographs can be scanned with a flatbed scanner, but not all flatbed scanners will handle transparencies or color negatives.

Resolution and color depth requirements should be considered. If the final goal is a printed product, the resolution of the scan will be the limit of the final printed output. Is 300-dpi good enough, or will you need 1200-dpi or more? Without adequate color depth, you may not end up with the desired range of colors.

You can use a histogram to compare the color output of different scanners. Histogram capability is included in many photo imaging software package, where they are used for analyzing the gray scale and colors of an image.

Does the scanner have software that allows corrections to be made before the image is scanned? This saves time and produces a much better quality image.

Finally, there is the challenge of determining how much disk memory will be needed to store the digitized images. A 300-dpi color scanner may create a 12-megabyte file per image, while the output from a high-resolution rotary-drum scanner may fill up 250 megabytes. A video image, on the other hand, may be as small as a half megabyte.

Rotary-Drum Scanners

Rotary-drum scanners offer the highest scanning resolution. The film or photograph is placed on the surface of a drum and is scanned by a beam of light while the drum rotates. The beam of light can be made larger or smaller, depending on the resolution desired. The light reflected from the image is detected by photomultipliers and is converted into digital signals.

Because of the rotation of the rotary drum scanner, very precise lines per millimeter can be achieved along with a spot size in which the image spot being read is of very, very fine form.

The typical rotary drum scanner uses a tungsten halogen light source with a beam size that can range anywhere from 1 to 1000 microns. The drum speed is variable as well. The resultant digital output, depending on the machine, can be from 8 bits to 14 bits per color.

Rotary-drum scanners require highly skilled operators. For that reason, and because of their high cost, rotary-drum scanners have been bought mainly by service bureaus and large printers. They are used to produce high-quality separations for four-color printing. Increasingly, today, service bureaus and printers are setting up links to their customers' desktop publishing systems. After the images are scanned, they provide their customers with "desktop" resolution versions of the scanned image for use in page layout then substitute the high-resolution image when the separations are made. Service bureaus also are offering sophisticated retouching and image manipulation capabilities to their customers.

Flatbed Scanners

Flatbed scanners are widely used in desktop publishing. The resolution of both monochrome and color flatbed scanners ranges from 200 to 1200 dots per inch. Unlike the

rotary-drum scanner, which scans with a single spot of light, a flatbed scanner scans an entire line at one time with a linear CCD array.

Flatbed scanners, for the most part, take reflective material up to 11 by 17 inches. Some will also handle transparent material up to 8 by 10 inches. Flatbed scanners are made by more than a dozen companies including Canon, Hewlett-Packard, Ricoh, Sharp, Imapro, and Sony to name a few (Figure 2-14). Most of the scanners come with software that allow you to determine the resolution, scanning area, file size, contrast, and other options.

There are some variations on the flatbed scanners. For example, the Chinon scanner looks like a copy stand (Figure 2-15). It uses a linear CCD array and a scanning mirror to scan the image at the base of the system. In a color version of this scanner, the operator has to manually insert filters in front of the scanning array.

A color scanner from Polaroid mechanically passes an inserted color print over a scanning head. The unit scans an image at 8 bits per color at either 500, 250, or 125 dpi.

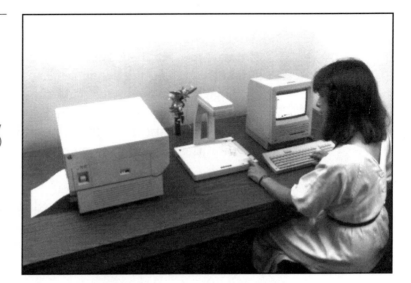

CREATING DIGITAL PHOTOGRAPHS

Film Scanners

The Leafscan was one of the earlier scanners for 35mm film. It has a 6000-dpi CCD linear array and provides an 8 bit per color output. It performs the analog to digital conversion internally, which means that its output is ready for computer use. Leafscan comes with a software package that operates the scanner, performs calibration, and provides for cropping and tone adjustments (Figure 2-16).

A widely used film scanner is made by Nikon. The Nikon film scanner makes a 2048 by 1356-pixel scan in 110 seconds, producing an 8.3 megabyte file. Images produced have 8 bits per color and a resolution of 5000 by 5000 pixels is possible. This scanner allows full rotation of the image with the film in its carrier.

A similar approach from Hasselblad provides a resolution of 3000 by 2000 pixels or the equivalent of 2200 dpi at 12 bits per color. The Barneyscan, another one of the original scanners, offers similar 35mm film scanning capabilities.

The Kodak 35mm film scanner takes a different approach.

Figure 2-16. The LeafScan 35 accepts mounted slides in portrait or landscape mode. (Courtesy Leaf Systems)

The Kodak scanner uses an area array that has a resolution of 1312 by 1024 pixels with an 8 bit per color resolution. Three successive exposures are made with red, green, and blue electronic flashes. A scan, with a total output of 4.2 megabytes, can be completed in a total of 15 seconds (Figure 2-17).

Figure 2-17. The Kodak 35 mm Rapid Film Scanner. (Courtesy Eastman Kodak Company)

A film scanner that fits into the half-drive slot of a personal computer has been developed by Current Limited. It provides a resolution of 3600 by 2400 pixels at 8 bits per color with a scanning time of three minutes for a full scan.

Tight Deadlines at *USA Today*

APPLICATION BRIEF

Still video solves the problem of tight deadlines in situations where color photos are required, says Frank Fallwell, assistant director of photography for USA Today *. The nation-wide newspaper uses an all-Sony video system from camera to prepress. The Sony 2-chip camera, combined with Sony's Digital Image Transceiver, make up a system for bringing pictures back from the field quickly. Using the SEPS system (Sony Electronic Publishing System), images are transferred directly to a Scitex image processor in only two minutes time.*

Video Cameras

Another way to capture an image is to use a video camera. There are some limitations, however. Video cameras usually operate at a level of 8 bits of RGB color, a basic limitation of the NTSC color signal.

Canon has made, for some time, the Video Visualizer, which has automatic focus, power zoom, exposure, and white light balance. As with most of the video cameras, the

Figure 2-18. The Fotovix can convert any 35mm or 2 1/4 inch film to video format. (Courtesy Tamron Industries, Inc.)

resolution is limited by the half-inch, 380,000-element CCD imaging device. For applications such as multimedia, the Visualizer proves to be entirely satisfactory.

Another approach to video capture of slides or negatives is found in the FotoVix produced by Tamron. The FotoVix converts 35mm or 2 1/4-inch negatives or positives for viewing on a TV screen. A version of the FotoVix is available from RasterOps as a personal slide scanner and another variation of the original FotoVix is available from Howtek as the Photomaster (Figure 2-18).

The Kodak SV5035 unit is designed for converting 35mm positive slides into a digital format for transfer to video-tape. The output is compatible with the NTSC television color standard and with the RGB color format used in personal computers. The unit has a motorized zoom and scan capability, allowing operators to position the slide image on a video screen and to display the entire image or the portion of interest.

After digitizing the slide images, the SV5035 can be used to output them to a variety of accessories, including the Kodak SV1300 color monitor, the Kodak SV7400 still-video recorder, and the Kodak SV6500 color video printer. The images can be transmitted over telephone lines, using Kodak still-video transceivers. The unit can also be used to output video images to standard video devices, including VCRs, monitors, optical disk recorders and framestores.

Figure 2-19. The Nikon HDTV camera produces a full 1125 line HDTV image. (Courtesy Nikon Inc.)

Higher resolution systems have also appeared for video capture. Fuji has shown an ultra-high resolution camera that uses three 800,000-pixel CCD sensors to produce an RGB image of commercial quality. The Nikon HDTV camera system produces an image of 1920 by 1035 pixels with 8 bits per color. A sequential RGB filter system provides color separations, but because of this filter system, 3/10 second is required for a single image (Figure 2-19).

Memory for Storing Digital Images

When we store digital photographs, we face the challenge of having to deal with a large amount of data. For example, an average color image may fill 10 or 12 megabytes, and a very high resolution image could be over 200 megabytes. In order to be able to handle such vast quantities of data, high-capacity memory systems are required.

While high capacity memory storage systems have been developed, a corresponding development also is helping to solve the problem of handling very large color image files. Compression and decompression of the data in color files can reduce the amount of memory needed by a factor of from five to one hundred. Compression-decompression chips and add-on boards are available (see Chapters Three and Six).

Three major memory technologies are available for storing digital image files. They are: magnetic, optical, and solid-state memory.

Magnetic Storage

Magnetic storage, thought by some as going out of style, still continues to be the major method of storage of both data and images.

Magnetic hard disk drives are getting faster and smaller, and at the same time their storage capacity is rising, up into the gigabyte range (that's a thousand megabytes).

The hard disk drives, 3 1/2-inch and 5 1/4-inch, can store 400 to 1200 megabytes with seek-times of 16.8 milliseconds and data transfer rates of 16.2 milliseconds. These high-capacity, high-performance disk drives offer the capabilities needed to handle large image files.

Another way to handle large amounts of image data is to

Figure 2-20. The TDK write once/read many times (WORM) optical disk can store 600 megabytes of digital information or images. (Courtesy TDK Electronics Corp.)

link up a number of standard hard disks in an array. These relatively inexpensive disk arrays can out-perform single drives of comparable capacity.

The digital audio tape (DAT) has found a place also as a storage medium for data and images. A DAT cartridge drive can replace a 3 1/2-inch disk drive on a personal computer. Each DAT cartridge can store 2 gigabytes, which means that it can handle several very high resolution images.

An older tape storage system uses a 9-track tape. The 9-track tape has become an accepted medium for the transfer of large color image files from one prepress system to another.

Optical Storage

Write-once optical disks have been useful in applications where it is important for information to be stored and not altered. For large-volume image storage, 12- and 14-inch optical disks, provide multi-gigabyte archival capacity. The more convenient 5 1/4-inch disks can be used for storage and retrieval of large volumes of images (Figure 2-20).

Optical tape recorders have been developed that can record up to 50 gigabytes per tape.

Figure 2-21. The Canon optical card system can hold 2 megabytes of memory on a credit-card size optical memory for read and write. (Courtesy Canon USA)

Optical memory card systems are another approach to storage. The Drexler optical memory card has been used for a variety of applications. It has a storage capacity of just under 3 megabytes. Japanese companies such as Canon and Dai Nippon Printing have take out licenses to produce optical memory cards (Figure 2-21).

Rewritable optical disks have also entered the market. While the early erasable optical storage systems were slow when compared to Winchester magnetic drives, these

Figure 2-22. Canon's complete MO-5001S, ready-to-use magneto-optical drive can write 256 megabytes to each 5 1/4-inch magneto-optical disk surface. (Courtesy Canon USA)

problems have been reduced to a point where the rewritable optical drives can compete in transfer times with magnetic storage.

The initial rewritable optical disk drives adopted the 5 1/4-inch format. (Figure 2-22). The increased speeds of the newer disks are partly due to the switch to the 3 1/2-inch format. This results in a reduction in the mass of all the various optical parts needed for the lasers and beam focusing.

The CD-ROM is another form of write-once storage material that can be used for a data distribution device. A number of manufacturers have produced computer drives for the CD-ROM, and pressing of the disks is done by major corporations including the many organizations that currently produce CD audio disks.

Sony has produced a 3 1/2-inch Data Discman. This pocket-size CD-ROM player has a liquid crystal screen and can store 200 megabytes of digital data, including text, graphics or a combination.

The Sony Mini-Disc has a 100-megabyte storage capacity and will play 64 minutes of audio. While not too much has been said about using either Data Discman or Mini-Disc for image storage, it would not be surprising to see one or both of these formats appear for other functions as well (Figure 2-23).

Figure 2-23. A prototype of the Sony Mini Disk player-recorder that can fit in a shirt pocket. (Courtesy Sony Corporation of America)

Electronic publishing, documentation, and archiving certainly are areas that will use mass storage of electronic files. Developers of software for corporate and government users have developed sophisticated programs for managing files that contain images. Image management software certainly will be a necessary tool for the the digital photographer.

Hybrid Photo-Digital System

Kodak's introduction of the Photo CD brought a hybrid product into the digital imaging marketplace. Photo CD starts with Kodak's traditional end products, slides and negatives, and gives the photographer the option to have them scanned and stored on a compact disk at the photofinishing lab. Using Kodak's Photo CD player, the photographer can display the photographs on a television screen, or by using a standard CD-ROM XA or CD-I drive, bring the digital photographs into his or her computer system (Figure 2-24).

Photo CD can store up to 100 color digital images that are scanned from 35mm film at about the same resolution as a 35mm negative—18 million pixels. Images are stored in a compressed form that was developed by Kodak. The images also can be stored in a decompressed form using a standard color space.

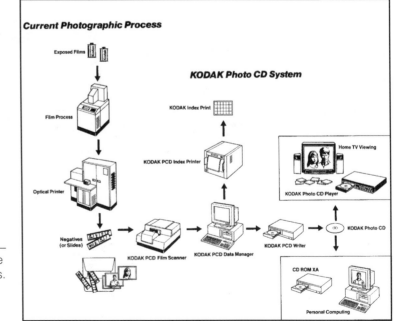

Figure 2-24. How the Kodak Photo CD works. (Courtesy Eastman Kodak Company)

Kodak has a strategic alliance with N.V. Philips for this project and that helps with the standardization problems. Already, the Photo CD can be used on the CD-ROM HA and CD-I players.

There are five resolutions available from each recorded image, ranging from 128 by 192-pixel proof-image to the full photo resolution of 2048 by 3072 pixels (compressed).

A Photo CD can store up to 100 images. The transfer of the images from film to disk will be done by the photofinishing lab. The equipment for the finisher includes a Kodak-developed scanner, a Sun Sparc workstation as the data manager, a Kodak XL-7700 printer to produce 42-image proof cards for the Photo CD boxes, and a CD optical disk writer from Philips. Kodak will make the optical disk and the materials for the printer (Figure 2- 25).

After the photographer slips the optical disk into the Photo CD player, he will be able to use a hand-held infrared control to select any image at random and then edit them

Figure 2-25. Kodak Photo CDs are compatible with NTSC, SECAM, PAL television, and also with HDTV formats. (Courtesy Eastman Kodak Company)

CREATING DIGITAL PHOTOGRAPHS

for position, zoom, and rotation; the unit remembers what was done by keeping track of the code number of the CD. The next time the CD is played, the player unit remembers the changes made and plays the image that way.

If that isn't enough, the player can also be used for CD audio disks. Photo CD can be used with American NTSC, European PAL, and SECAM television sets, and current version of Japanese HDTV.

Initial application of the Photo CD is expected to be in commercial areas, for example in catalog production where it will be possible to have available 100 full-color high-resolution on a single CD, and others made available simply by changing the CD. Images on Photo CD are suitable for importing into the various color software photo packages that are used for manipulating images and positioning them on a page.

The Photo CD system has also been used in conjunction with the new CDI systems from Philips and the CDTV interactive multimedia from Commodore for interactive playback.

Kodak will make "open licenses for the products" available to other manufacturers at reasonable fees.

Tass News Agency Tries Electronic Cameras

APPLICATION BRIEF

Moscow-based Tass news agency is trying out 10 Sony Mavica still video cameras for fast-breaking stories. Images are to be transmitted directly to pressrooms or other locations for computer processing. The electronic cameras eliminate the need for film developing.

Solid State Memory and Memory Cards

There is nothing faster in image memory than solid-state memory. A number of attempts have been made to create solid state memory devices that would permit storage of large image files, but usually the cost has been too high except for military and intelligence applications. The advantage of a solid-state memory for images is that it would be displayed instantly.

Recent memory cards for digital still-video image cameras have only reached a four-digit price level for a single card. But there is still hope.

A touch memory has been developed that is enclosed in a 16mm container, which looks much like the tiny flat batteries used in electronic clocks and other devices. Even the holder for the touch memory looks like a battery holder. The first touch memory units were able to store 4096 bits.

Another development is a 2 1/2-inch form factor memory from Sundisk Corp. that stores 20.9 megabytes. Seagate has developed a solid-state disk drive that can store up to 167 megabytes. If this isn't enough, Vermont Research Ltd. has created a solid-state disk drive that can store as much as 1 gigabyte using 1-megabit or 4-megabit DRAMs. Designed with the SCSI interface, the VMI system can be daisy-chained up to 7 gigabytes and when you think of image storage, that becomes very attractive.

The memory cards first seen in games have found a practical market the laptop computers. A 68-pin standard will allow standardization of both software and configuration, and should bring the cost of these cards down dramatically. One example is Poqet Computer's PC. The 1.2 pound PC offers 64 and 512 kilobyte memory cards and will run up to 100 hours on two AA batteries—thanks to solid-state storage. While the capacity of this memory card is not enough for many imaging functions, it looks as if the memory card for the portable computers will be useful for some of the needs in the photo imaging area as well. There are predictions that memory cards will reach 1 gigabyte in size by the year 2000.

CREATING DIGITAL PHOTOGRAPHS

CHAPTER 3

Processing Digital Photographs

The processing of digital photographs does not take place in a darkroom, but rather in a darkened room (so the colors on the screen are more accurately perceived). Replacing the developers, fixers, enlargers, filters, and other paraphernalia of the darkroom is the computer, color monitor, and color printer or imagesetter.

The real processing magic is found in the computer software that gives the user the power to manipulate and change not only the colors and size of the image, but also change the image itself into something new, or merge it with other digital images. It is possible to produce altered images of such high quality that can be aptly called second-generation originals.

The digital darkroom requires a high-resolution display screen that can accurately and rapidly present the image. Digital images can be returned to film simply using a color printer or imagesetter and outputting on film. With the emergence of a nearly universal page description language, PostScript, digital images can be sent directly to a wide variety of devices.

For processing digital images, you will need additional memory for your computer, both RAM memory and disk memory for storage. Since all the information is digital, the processing is very heavily weighed toward the arithmetic processing of individual pixels. Use of math co-processors and accelerator boards increase the efficiency of a computer that is doing image processing.

New boards have been created that accelerate and automate many of the imaging processes. Most of the more powerful personal computers and workstations allow multitasking, which enables more than one operation to run at the same time. So while the computer is making a global change that may take several minutes, the operator can continue to work on another task.

Optimizing the system in terms of hardware and software will produce the best results, which is why there is a ready market for dedicated systems.

In this book, we have chosen to separate the digital processing system from the page make-up system. It is becoming very clear that these two systems will become one in the future. But today, let's take a closer look at the components of an image processing system.

Several Levels of Service for Computer Imaging

APPLICATION BRIEF

Service laboratories now offer levels of digital photography services. At DugalColor Projects in New York, Mac Imaging is designed for continuous tone transparencies from files created by photographers on their own computers or digital scans from 35mm to 4 x 5 originals. The computer imaging is high-resolution film scanning and film recording for electronic retouching, photo composition, and special effects.

Graphic and Image Processing Boards

At AT&T's Electronic and Photographic Imaging Center (EPICenter), an "intrapreneurial" venture was launched in 1984. A few years later the "intrapreneurial" employees purchased the operation from AT&T and renamed it Truevision Inc. The company had produced the Targa image-capture board, also known as a frame grabber or a digitizer. The board could take a color image from a video source and immediately display it on a computer screen. The Targa board quickly became recognized as one of the best color image digitizers for PCs. Several hundred third-party companies offer imaging software that utilizes the Targa boards.

Truevision continues to develop new image processing boards. The NuVista video graphic boards are for the Macintosh, and the ATVista boards are for AT computers. The Vista boards digitize color images at 8, 16, or 32 bits per pixel. They have up to 4 megabytes of video memory and are compatible with NTSC or PAL (Figure 3-1).

Many other companies make imaging boards for the PC or the Macintosh computers. The important consideration is whether the software you plan to use is compatible with the digital processing board you plan to buy.

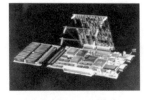

Figure 3-1. The Truevision NuVista+ transforms the Apple Macintosh II into a video and graphic workstation. (Courtesy Truevision)

The function of the video graphics display board found in computers is to allow a hardware interface between the program and the actual screen. This consists of a special video memory and digital-to-analog converter, frequently called a DAC, which transforms the digital value associated with each pixel into an equivalent analog value ranging from pixel-color-off to pixel-color-on.

The number of colors that each pixel can display is determined by the number of bits per pixel. If the system uses 8-bits per color, then it can generate a total of 16.7 million different colors. However, most computer screens can show only 256 different color at one time. The user selects the color ranges that are to be displayed, and can change the selection. All this is done with chips called RAM-DAC, which are used to support a color look-up table (CLUT) and three DACs.

The lookup table runs the 256 colors on the screen, while the DACs do the conversion of the digital signals to analog signals, which are then sent to the electron guns of the monitor.

For image processing, it is best if the screen has a high resolution. On PCs, the standard VGA display provides 256 colors with a resolution of 320 by 200 pixels. An enhanced VGA mode provides the same number of colors but with 640 by 480 pixels. For high-resolution color work, a 1000 by 1000 screen is used and each color is 6- to 8- bits deep. High-resolution monitors and their graphics boards are expensive. TIGA displays have a potential resolution of 4000 by 4000 pixels (Figure 3-2).

Figure 3-2. Graphic display standards.

Display Resolutions		
Standard	**Resolution (pixels)**	**Number of Colors**
VGA	320 x 200	256
	640x480	2 or 16
SuperVGA	640x400	256
	800x600	16 or 256
	1024x768	16 or 256
	1280x1024	16
8514A (IBM-MCA)	640x480	256
	1024x768	16 or 256
XGA	640x480	256 or 65,536
	1024x768	256
TIGA	4000x4000 (max)	16.7 million

Most people probably saw their first computer-processed images in the 1960s when pictures from space probes began to appear in newspapers and on television. The signals transmitted from space required substantial processing and enhancement, and this work was pioneered at the Jet Propulsion Laboratory (JPL) of the California Institute of Technology. Many of the basic image processing techniques developed by JPL have been carried over into software for personal computers.

There are a variety of capture boards for image processing. In addition to capture and display boards, there are digital-input frame grabbers, variable-scan frame grabbers, and real-time video digitizers. As the name implies, real-time digitizers take a video field and immediately convert it to a digital signal. When you are working with a CCD sensor or a digital camera instead of a video sensor, an asynchronous digital video digitizer is useful for handling the serial digital stream.

There is also the combination capture and display board, which offers video output capability as well as capture. The output signal can be an RS-170, CCIR or RGB. The boards provide 512 by 512 or 640 by 480 interlaced display resolution. While these boards are typically NTSC or PAL compatible, they are usually not compatible with VGA or standard display formats. If these boards have RGB outputs, they may be found with look-up tables and digital-to-analog converters. An example of this type of board is the Targa board from Truevision.

Chips Make the Difference

What made possible the growth of imaging and graphics boards was the advent of a series of chips designed specifically for imaging applications. With the boost given by graphic chips and boards, today's PCs and Macs can attain levels of image processing that a decade ago could be done only on mainframes and supercomputers.

The original PC graphics boards provided what is called pseudocolor, which uses 8-bit planes and a maximum of 256 colors. With 24-bit true color, over 16 million color combinations are possible. There are still some problems that future chip designs will have to overcome before true color implementation is fully developed.

The original VGA resolution of 640 by 480 wasn't really a problem until users started displaying large photographic images or several images. When you start using a resolution of 1080 by 1024, you are moving a lot more pixels (Figure 3-3). Graphic subsystems will be necessary to handle greatly increasing burdens, and so will higher speed RAM-DACs. Another way to increase processing speed is to use video RAM instead of dynamic RAM, although the cost may be higher.

Digital signal processing chips (DSP) are also increasing in power and speed. The number crunching of these devices has increased substantially with extra capability such as better memory addressing and improved I/O capabilities, leading to more efficient construction of processing boards.

Figure 3-3. Analog Devices ADV7140 series CEG/DACs extends apparent resolution of 320 by 200-pixel PC monitors to 1280 by 1024 pixels, and expands the color palette from 256 to nearly 800,000. (Courtesy Analog Devices)

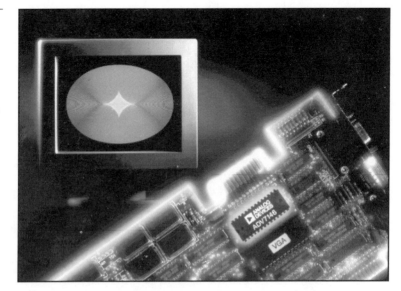

Microprocessor chips have been increasing in their processing speed, with some companies achieving 50 MHz. When you look at the microprocessor that is found at the heart of most of today's personal computers, you find an amazing array of technology that controls and synchronizes all the information that is being processed to and from memory as well as in the chip. What is most amazing is that to operate this vast factory of operations requires less electricity than it takes to light a flashlight bulb.

Becoming Another Person

APPLICATION BRIEF

A commercial system called PhotoMagic brings a graphic workstation together with images of famous people so that one person's face can be transposed to another body and produced either as a magazine cover, poster-sized image, or transferred to posters, T-shirts, pillows, and souvenirs.

Processing Platforms for the Digital Darkroom

After a digital image has been created, it then passes into the realm of the computer. For the photographer, the computer may actually become the digital darkroom, where images can be enlarged and cropped, retouched, and otherwise manipulated.

It wasn't long ago that image processing had to be done on a very large minicomputer with an extraordinary amount of memory and at prices which could range from six to seven figures. Now there is an abundance of choices in processing platforms, ranging from personal computers to Risc workstations with Unix-based software.

Desktop image processing began to happen in earnest with

Figure 3-4. The Macintosh IIfx integrates a number of powerful technologies. (Courtesy Apple Computer)

the arrival of the Macintosh II—it was the preferred choice for many who processed and enhanced digital photographs. Most popular among the new series was the Macintosh IIfx (Figure 3-4).

The limitation of the Macintosh computer is still the bus that carries information through the computer, much like an electrical distribution system carries electricity to our homes. The NuBus architecture on the Macintosh was not intended to carry large volumes of data and it limits the speed of information transfer, as does the Mac's SCSI input interface (Figure 3-5).

An interim solution is the dash30fx workstation from Sixty Eight Thousand Inc., which accelerates the Macintosh to 50 MHz. For storage-intensive applications such as imaging, the dash30fx workstation's 10 half-height drive slots can incorporate as much as 10 gigabytes of storage.

Apple's operating System 7 has added features that are helpful for digital photograph processing. Multitasking is

Figure 3-5.
Comparison of bus architectures.

Bus	ISA	EISA	MCA	NuBus
Bus Speed	2.5 MB/s	33MB/s	20 MB/s 40 MB/s (32-bit)	2.5 MB/s

built in so that you can switch from a page layout software to image-enhancement software with just one mouse click. The System 7 virtual memory allows for larger programming. The use of 32-bit addressing improves the speed of image processing by allowing the operating system to quickly reach large amounts of RAM.

The more powerful PCs finding great application in the area of digital photography. Since the advent of Windows 3.0 software from Microsoft, a number of PC image enhancement and publishing programs for digital photographs have appeared and are offering some interesting advantages. With a choice of the EISA bus or MCA bus, it is possible to transfer data at up to 33 megabytes per second. The Hewlett-Packard Vectra 486 uses the EISA bus (Figure 3-6).

With the addition of parallel processing boards using the Intel i860, it is possible to increase the speed of the PC to 120 MIPS, which begins to approach supercomputer speeds.

With memories becoming faster and less costly, there was a need to shorten the amount of time needed to cycle instructions. The answer was the reduced instruction, or Risc, microprocessor, which contains many of the needed instructions within the microprocessor.

One of the first Risc-based computers was from Sun, and today more than a dozen Unix computers based on Sun Microsystem's scalable processor architecture (Sparc) have appeared from names such as GoldStar, Hyundai, Tatung and others.

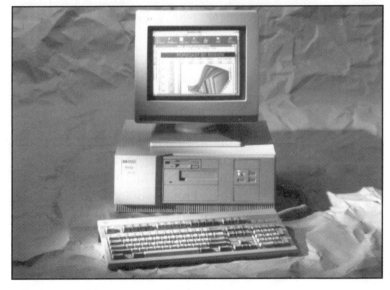

Figure 3-6. The EISA-based HP Vectra 486s/20 PC from Hewlett-Packard uses the 20 MHz Intel 486SX, a next generation graphic accelerator for greater power and flexibility. (Courtesy Hewlett-Packard Company)

Sun workstations have been the engines of choice for image enhancement systems such as the Kodak Premier Image Enhancement System. Sun has a significant portion of the Unix workstation market in the electronic design area.

IBM's approach to Risc processing is the RS/6000 workstation. The System/6000 uses a 32-bit Micro Channel Architecture. Even the lowest level unit provides 120 megabytes of fixed disk with 8 megabytes of RAM memory.

Electronic Still Cameras and Art

APPLICATION BRIEF

Artist Laurence M. Gartel is a founding instructor of computer art at the School of Visual Arts in New York City. He likes to work with still video, specifically the Canon system. Images can be input directly into his computer, saved for future work with Photoshop and ColorStudio to create new images, changes, or elaborations of the original work. Gartel particularly likes the immediacy of the system and the ability to edit and erase images he no longer needs.

Image-Enhancement Software

The availability of image enhancement software has probably done more to stimulate interest in digital photography than anything else.

The new software packages not only modify and enhance photographs, but also assist in the control of input and output devices. The variety of available software packages is particularly attractive.

The first retouching packages available were gray-scale programs for monochrome images, but today most programs can efficiently handle 24- and 32-bit color images of almost any size.

Adobe Systems' Photoshop was not the first Macintosh image-editing software package, but it has become, for many people, an answer to their dreams for retouching. Photoshop allows photo retouching, image manipulation, color correction of both contrast and brightness, the production of color separations, and even the creation of original art work.

The RubberStamp of Photoshop allows an image to be cloned onto other parts of the same or different image (Figure 3-7). For example, a rose may be combined with the petals from a tulip to create an entirely new flower. By controlling the opacity of the revert function, ghost images can be created with any degree of transparency. Like most packages, Photoshop allows feathering of edges so that a smooth look can be achieved in retouching, like that found in the work of professional retouchers.

Input into Photoshop can be a scanned photograph, slide, or illustration, or an image file created by other means, such as still video and digital cameras. It is possible to blend, layer, or otherwise use multiple images for mosaic or

Figure 3-7. The rubber stamp tool in Adobe Photoshop allows the user to clone items in the photograph.

photorealistic or impressionistic effects. With the use of virtual memory, it is possible to work with practically any image on the normal Macintosh. Support is provided for a dozen different formats including encapsulated PostScript, TIFF, and Scitex.

ColorStudio from Fractal Design(Figure 3-8) provides for such things as 1 percent incremental adjustments of images that have been scanned. Colors can be selected from a full range of Pantone colors, while at the same time you can skew, stretch, move, rotate, scale, and tilt images.

Several software packages are available for Windows version 3. Picture Publisher Plus provides gray-scale editing, image retouching, masking, and most of the enhancement functions.

PhotoStyler from Aldus takes advantage of Windows 3 with features such as an easy-user interface, palette control, virtual memory, and multi-document interface (MDI). Multiple images may be displayed at the same time or in as many windows with different zoom-in and zoom-out scales.

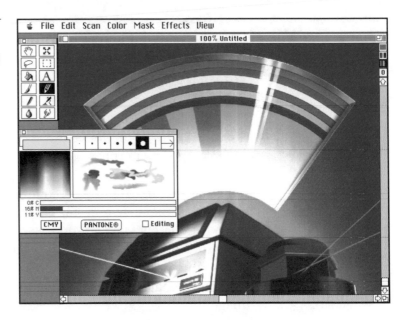

Figure 3-8. Fractal Design's ColorStudio was originally marketed by Letraset.

With virtual memory, there is no limit to the size of images. PhotoStyler supports a variety of imaging peripheral devices and popular file formats such as TIFF, TGA, EPSP, CX, BMP, and GIF. Data interchange may also be done using the PhotoStyler software.

Image-In-Color from Image-In Inc. makes an interesting use of the right mouse button in Windows 3. The right button controls the size, density, and pressure of tools such as paint brush, airbrush, pencil, and others. Extensive use of filter controls and input and output support makes Image-In-Color a useful tool.

With IMS color, from VI and C Technology, up to 10 image windows can be opened simultaneously.

When you look at the capabilities of a typical software package available today, you see the tremendous strides that have been made in software giving the ability that once was only in the domain of the large workstation to the Macintosh, IBM PC, or compatible.

How Do Workstations Fit In?

Although PCs and Macintosh computers are more widely used, minicomputer-based workstations are attractive for high-end applications such as prepress and retouching. Some of workstations being offered today rival supercomputers in their processing power.

Image processing requires a combination of speed, large amounts of memory and, for color, the ability to handle three completely separate pieces of information in total synchronization. While this has been solved by the variety of new imaging boards, there are still photo-application systems being developed dedicated to the handling of images.

In many cases, the limitation of the use of the workstation platform is software availability, where software for the individual platform has not been developed because the platform has not been used in a digital photography application.

IBM has introduced the ImagePlus concept of imaging, which can handle both documents and photographs. Much more can be expected in the way of software to support digital photography applications on the workstations being developed by IBM.

Workstations have been the basis for many of the older systems used for satellite imaging and medical photography. In recent years, a number of companies have developed minicomputer-based design stations, imaging workstations, and prepress workstations. For example, the Sun workstation is used as part of the Kodak Premier Retouching System.

Sun, DEC, Hewlett-Packard, and Sony, to name a few of the workstation companies, are all actively looking at additional applications for their systems, particularly in the prepress and document imaging areas. The use of these same workstations for digital photography is limited by the lack of software more than anything else.

Creating a New Reality

◆

APPLICATION BRIEF

Advertising photographer Eric Meola uses the Macintosh II to create new images. Starting out with a Barneyscan slide scanner, he combines several images to create a new image. His belief is that ultimately photography will become "first shoot the picture, then manipulate it for final result" and that having the second stage will help create a better image than could be obtained with a single camera image.

Packaged Image Enhancement Systems

Less than a decade ago, a complete image enhancement system was a million dollar investment and required a team of skilled technicians to operate. So it's not surprising that most continued to use the traditional brush or air gun art of the retoucher.

Today a number of excellent systems are available that include platform software and hardware along with options for input scanning and image outputting in the form of either tape or hard copy print or film images.

Most of these systems are found with two separate monitors, one a high resolution color monitor, usually at the 1000-line level or higher, and the other a black-and-white screen to display the software commands. Just a few years ago, efforts were made to bring all of the controls in front of

Figure 3-9. Left to right: Optronics ColorGetter Scanner, a Dicomed Imaginator SI Imaging Workstation, and a Dicomed Captivator Film Camera. (Courtesy Dicomed Inc.)

the system operator. Now a graphical user screen interface is often provided or a touch-sensitive tablet is used to call up commands as well as to input modifications functions on the tablet which can be touched with a stylus to indicate the function being called for (Figure 3-9).

While the old, expensive Crosfield, Hell, and Scitex systems are still used in many areas, today names such as Agfa, Barco, Graphix, Dicomed, Kodak, ImageMax, Imapro, Intergraph, Management Graphics, Networked Picture Systems, and SuperSet are a reasonable cross section of the the companies offering packaged image enhancement systems. Their systems can perform not only image enhancement, but also can add type to images for creating advertisements. They also can be used to create new photographic originals.

What most of these systems have in common is the ability to input a variety of images from different sources, including rotary-drum, flatbed, slide, and even video sources, and then output these to magnetic tape or directly to color printers and imagesetters.

The workstation systems provide high-quality retouching

capability, and all would be effective for digital photo retouching. Most use RAM memory so that a portion of the image can be enlarged for retouching (Color Figure 3-10).

The Kodak Premier System employs some uniquely designed technology. The scanner module uses Kodak's 8000-element CCD, which are arranged in three rows and that have integrated filters selected for a narrow wavelength transmission. The Kodak Premier FilmWriter provides a resolution of 1000 pixels per inch on an 8 by 10 inch sheet film through the use of a PLZT crystal.

While the features of each of the individual retouching systems have variations, the quality output of these systems is outstanding. The difference is in individual unit capabilities such as the speed of the system, functions such as warping, and the size of the image display (Color Figure 3-11).

Retail Digital Imaging Design Center

APPLICATION BRIEF

Imageland is a retail digital imaging design center located in Chicago and features the latest computerized color imaging equipment put together as a network. A Dicomed Imaginator SI Image Workstation is used for retouching, color changes, masking, image assembly, line art/text stripping, image rotation, and fake color tinting functions. Input scanning is everything from customer artwork to 35mm slides with output to Canon laser copiers, Kodak thermal digital printers, Canon, and Iris inkjet printers.

Image Compression

A digital photographic image is likely to have a great deal of redundancy where the same information appears more than once. When there are patches of the same color in different parts of the image, this may be one type of redundancy. Straight lines, for example, create another type of redundancy. We can take advantage of this redundancy in order to save storage space by compressing the original image (Color Figure 3-12).

We can identify three types of redundancies. These are:

- Spatial redundancy—a correlation (dependence) among neighboring pixel values.

- Spectral redundancy—a correlation of color planes (RGB) or spectral bands.

- Temporal redundancy—a correlation between different frames in a sequence of images.

A standard for image compression is being developed by the Joint Photographic Experts Group (JPEG) combines a technique called discrete cosine transform (DCT), adaptive quantization, and Huffman coding. The technique allows the user to select the compression ratio—generally, the higher the ratio, the lower the quality.

As the quality of an electronic still image improves, so does the size of the computer file generated for that image. The key to the future of digital electronic photography will be the ability to compress image files. Compressed files will be easier to store and transmit. But there is a risk that as you increase the compression of your image, data is lost and the integrity of your image is compromised.

Compression of images depends on the redundancy of information in the image. Images may be compressed because of the dependence of each pixel value on the value of its neighbors. The larger this dependence, the more compression is achievable.

The information content of images depends on the resolution, noise level, bit depth, and many other things and is difficult to quantify. We refer to images as lossless when the reconstructed pixel values are identical to the original values. Lossless algorithms can usually provide compression ratio of up to 5 to 1. With lossy compression, some discrepancies will occur between the original and reconstructed pixel values.

Image compression will be meaningful in the development of multimedia as well as in the growing field of document and image storage. The advent of the JPEG standard will open a major path for standardization on a worldwide basis.

Four years of work by JPEG were required to produce a color image data compression standard ready for international balloting.

Initially, some 12 proposals were registered as candidates for the compression method. The field was narrowed to three techniques—adaptive discrete cosine transform (DCT), differential pulse code modulation with adaptive arithmetic coding, and progressive block truncation.

From test results it became clear that DCT produced better quality pictures than the other contenders did and it was selected as the world standard.

The DCT standard actually is a family of image compression techniques rather than a single compression technique. The toolkit consists of four modes. The sequential DCT-based mode of operation image components are coded separately, and the data and coding operations are interleaved.

Progressive DCT mode is achieved by a sequence of scans in which 64 DCT coefficients for each 8 by 8 block are decomposed in one or both of two complementary ways—spectral selection and successive approximation.

The JPEG algorithm has three main components: a simple DCT-based algorithm that is adequate for most image encoding applications; an optional extended system with optional provisions for 12-bit/pixel input, hierarchical and sequential progressive build-up, and arithmetic coding; and a simple DPCM-based lossless method independent of DCT for lossless compression.

Image compression has become easier with the advent of DCT chips from LSI Logic, SGS-Thomson Microelectronics, C-Cube, Zoran, and others.

A number of board-level products have been developed to support the JPEG standard. The Alice-ISA image compression board handles 8- to 32-bit color images with selectable compression parameters of good, better, best, and perfect, making it simple for the user to select the final quality of the compressed image.

The Rapid Technology Visionary board has been produced using the LSI Logic compression chip (Figure 3-13). Fuji Photo Film is using the Zoran chip in their digital still video camera.

Figure 3-13. The Rapid Technology Visionary Compression Board handles JPEG compression. (Courtesy Rapid Technology Corp.)

Other boards are available from Optibase which has released their Compex with available compression and expansion algorithms, including JPEG and lossless.

Optipac produces image compression for both PCs and IBM Micro Channel computers. The Optipac Series 250 board can compress a 512 by 416-bit image in less than one second.

Storm Technology offers a PicturePress accelerator card

for use in image compression along with PicturePress 2.0, which operates under the Apple 7.0 operating system.

Not all manufacturers are sticking with the JPEG. Ricoh has developed a proprietary system that is called the Generalized Chen Transform (GCT). Ricoh indicates that its image compression is 30 percent faster than other systems. With the GCT technology, the multiplications needed to process a color image are reduced from a current 150 to 64.

Development efforts on the Intel DVI product promises the potential of another competing technology for practical video compression. These systems allow compression from 5 to 1 all the way to 220 to 1, with the user selecting the quality loss they are willing to accept in the final image.

Iterated Images has shown examples of fractal image compression of both still and video images as an alternative to DCT.

Image compression will be very important to multimedia images and CD-ROMs that employ many hundreds of still and video images as part of their material.

Electronic Photography for Package Design

**APPLICATION
BRIEF**

Proctor-Silex Inc. relied on outside design agencies until electronic still cameras from Sony combined with design stations allowed the work to be brought in-house. The results were a savings of time and expense, particularly in making changes in the design after the initial stages.

PROCESSING DIGITAL PHOTOGRAPHS

CHAPTER 4

Publishing Digital Photographs

After digital photographs that are destined for the printed page have been created, the operations move from the digital darkroom into desktop publishing. Physically, the move may consist of clicking a mouse button to switch the computer from the imaging software to page layout software, or it may involve moving to a desktop publishing or prepress workstation.

Electronic prepress, the way printers get materials ready for printing presses, is not new, but the traditional way of doing it is being replaced by desktop publishing (DTP).

There may be some confusion as to where DTP fits in. Graphic designers have gained direct control over page layout, for the most part doing it themselves on screen. Service bureaus, which used to do some of the work now done by DTP software, are finding new ways to stay in the production loop.

While the first programs for desktop publishing were black-and-white, today the demand for color hardware and software is exploding. Most Fortune 1000 companies have standardized their desktop color systems with color monitors. Those color systems are intended for handling color pages with color images—a ready market for digital photographers.

Desktop Publishing Software

It seems that every day improved versions of desktop publishing software or additional vendors appear. In addition, packages that were originally designed only for text editing have become more powerful and allow users to create complete pages.

Desktop publishing programs vary widely in their capabilities. Inexpensive software packages are suited mostly for producing flyers and other simple one-page documents. More expensive DTP software packages include features such as sophisticated typographic controls, direct control of scanning, image enhancement and retouching, and color controls.

There are a number of software packages that allow users, on their desktop, to integrate type and digital photographs. PageMaker from Aldus Corp. was one of the early packages on the Macintosh (Figure 4-1). Ventura Publisher was one of the first packages for the IBM PC. QuarkXPress has

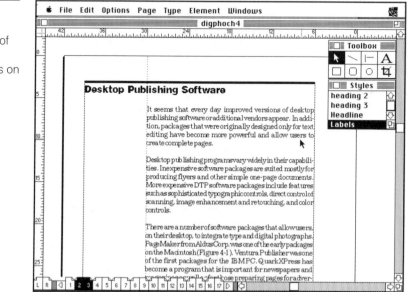

Figure 4-1. Aldus PageMaker for the Macintosh was one of the first desktop publishing programs on the market.

become a program that is important for newspapers and magazines as well as for those preparing pages for advertising (Figure 4-2).

The real difference in the various available software packages comes when you attempt to bring a variety of type, digitized color or black-and-white photographs, and other variations of spot color or patterns to a finished printed page.

Common to most of the page layout programs is their text editing, and layout capabilities, and their typographic controls, which have become almost as sophisticated as those found in dedicated typesetting systems.

Page layout programs have been augmented with capabilities such as generating full-color separations and control of the final printing output.

Aldus PrePrint is one of the products designed to allow linkage, image enhancement and printing options (Figure 4-3). While it is compatible with files from PageMaker,

Figure 4-2.
QuarkXPress is popular among creative professionals using the Macintosh.

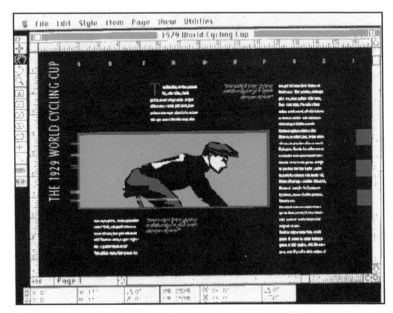

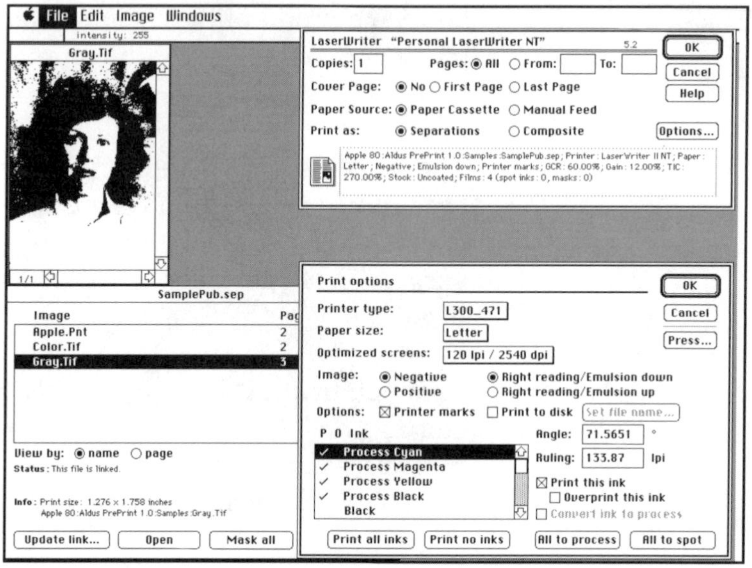

Figure 4-3. Aldus PrePrint manages the process of producing color separations from desktop publishing programs.

Freehand and Adobe Illustrator, it also accommodates TIFF (Tag Image Format File), DCS (Desktop Color Separation), and Paint files. Aldus PageMaker now serves both the needs of the Macintosh and the IBM PC user with Windows 3.

Ventura software, one of the earliest of the page make-up software programs for the IBM PC and compatible computers has moved to a Microsoft Windows-base. In its latest version, Ventura has added four color prepress products—Ventura Scan, Ventura Separator, Ventura PhotoTouch and Ventura ColorPro—that allow seamless integration of color scanning, separation, and photo editing.

Ventura Scan allows scanning of black-and-white, gray scale, or color images directly from within Ventura Publisher. Up to 16 scanning devices are accessible.

Ventura Separator produces CYMK separations of complete pages with all text, graphics and continuous tone color images in place. It corrects for such things as printing press dot gain and provides for halftone screen angles.

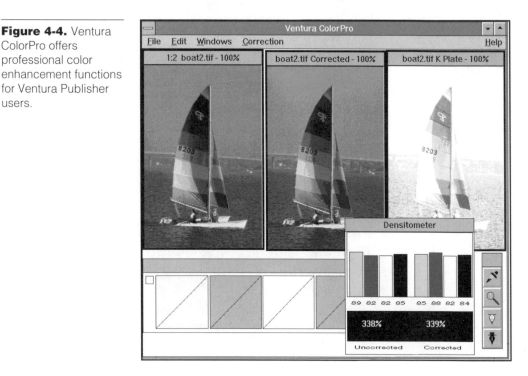

Figure 4-4. Ventura ColorPro offers professional color enhancement functions for Ventura Publisher users.

PhotoTouch provides a range of creative tools to outline, air brush, sharpen, blur, blend, smear, lighten or darken, shift hue, shift saturation, add or subtract color and gradation.

Ventura ColorPro provides professional control of the high-end drum scanner in an approachable Windows environment (Figure 4-4). It provides for such functions as undercolor removal (UCR), which reduces ink densities and shadow tones as needed by specific printing presses. Its undercolor addition (UCA) controls neutral shadow densities without affecting colors in the image. GCR (gray component replacement) maintains the color balance in neutral grays by replacing process inks with black inks. These are some of the more sophisticated tools of the color stripper, but now available for desktop use.

QuarkXPress has been described in one headline as the "darling" of ad agencies and magazines. The reason for the attention is that XPress manipulates color photographs, graphics, and text in a way that is precisely suitable for the high-quality standards of magazines. The software has also found use at a number of newspapers because of its ability to put together complete pages with type and pictures all in register.

With QuarkXPress, trapping is done automatically, but complete operator control is available. The system checks trapping values for the object color relative to background color and uses the minimum of these values.

Page Geometry

Important with all of these programs is page geometry. More important are the typographic issues: kerning, tracking, leading, and font calls. These are some of the basic things you need to get good typography. There have been very few programs that address these issues and also take care of the page geometry.

Kerning is intercharacter spacing on a character pair basis. An example is a capital T and a lower case o. This combination requires kerning to pull the o underneath the umbrella of the T.

Tracking is the overall letter spacing within a line or paragraph. When you take all the tracking that is available to you, you actually reduce the space between all the characters. The emphasis, for example, that QuarkXPress has been able to put on good typography has helped to give it a lead in the marketplace.

Page geometry is a unique issue. If you are simply printing on plain paper, page geometry is not important. You can do an 8 1/2 by 11-inch page with standard format that most people will recognize and accept. But once you go to the printing press, you will have to allow for bleed, that portion of the page that will be trimmed or cut in the finishing of the page. You have to identify the active page area with crop marks, and also put in color registration and other information.

Think of an artist working on an easel. Your picture is going to be actually within the easel. Within that picture geometry you will have some other things. This frame within a frame concept is an important part of page geometry.

It's important that you understand these definitions. If you just hand a file over to your service bureau, typesetter, or printer, you may not get the page size you expected. Or you may be paying for more film than you really have to.

Trapping Color

One of the real challenges of color printing of photographs or artwork is making sure that no white space appears where two colors touch. This can be in a four-color illustration or a simple one-color block. This control is achieved through trapping, a standardized technique that allows for the slight shift and stretch of paper as it passes through the printing press.

The real trick in trapping is to allow just enough overlap to compensate for any gaps created by misregistration, paper stretch, or other press problems. The traditional way traps are created is by a photomechanical expansion or shrinkage of the edge of the color area by .003 inches or .25 point before the plates are produced.

Enlarging the outline of the foreground object is called spreading, while shrinking the whole color image under an object is called choking. This technique has now been applied in varying degrees of capability in most software programs that offer color imaging.

Low-Resolution Files

A desktop system cannot always handle the entire file for a color image scanned at high resolution. The file is just too big. So how do you handle page layout when you are using high-resolution scans?

One approach is to scan the image again on a 300-dpi

scanner, and use the image file for positioning and cropping. But that leaves out the all important color control functions.

To address this problem, vendors of high-end scanners have developed links to desktop publishing systems. One such link, Scitex' Visionary, takes the high-resolution scan, samples it, and passes a low-resolution version to the desktop system. This approach allows you to have a more manageable four-color image in your system and yet gain the effectiveness of a high-end system. When it comes time to produce separations, Visionary applies the changes made to the low-resolution file to the high-resolution file.

Until recently, the ability to handle and manipulate photo images has been the domain of the color craftsman in color separations. The craftsman learned from experience when he had to shoot "fatties" or "skinnies" and desktop publishers are finding out that they also have to learn the tricks of the trade from experience.

In many of the early page layout programs, the biggest problem was for the user to get the desired results. Newer systems such as Visionary addressed that with their gateway system—much of the work became automatic. There still is a need for users to understand the technology that is available to them today.

Desktop Publishing PC Magazine

APPLICATION BRIEF

The PC has generally taken a back seat as a page make-up tool to the Macintosh. PC Magazine, on the other hand, has used the PC as its hardware standard. Before switching to desktop, covers cost $5000 to separate and produce. The first electronically published cover of PC Magazine with in-house separations cost just $80, demonstrating what can be done.

Working with PostScript

Adobe's PostScript has become almost a de facto standard for the outputting of printed pages. Even the latest computer-to-press technology, where pages are sent directly to a press cylinder, uses the PostScript page description language.

PostScript Files for Output

If you plan to produce your documents at a service bureau, you will probably get to know the PostScript file format very well. Unless you use the service bureau's publishing software to produce your publications, you will probably create your document on your own computer, print it to disk as a PostScript file, and take it to the service bureau. There it will be downloaded to the imagesetter and produced at high resolution.

When you create a PostScript file from a desktop publishing or graphics package, the software is actually writing a PostScript program. All text and images on the page are converted into PostScript commands by means of a PostScript driver. Usually this driver interacts directly with the printer, but it can also produce PostScript output in the form of a disk file.

File Sizes

One problem with these files is that they tend to be big. PostScript is extremely economical in the commands it uses to describe an image, but it still takes a lot of English-like instructions to draw a picture. This holds true for pages that consist mostly of text, but the biggest PostScript files are those that contain graphic images, especially bit-mapped images in color or multiple shades of gray.

To understand why this is so, remember that a bit-mapped image consists of tiny dots. If it is a scanned image, it might have as many as 300 dpi, which translates into 90,000 dots in a square inch. An image measuring 2 by 3 inches would thus contain 540,000 dots. Now suppose you have a gray-scale image in which each dot can be any one of 256 shades of gray. It takes eight bits of information — one byte — to describe each dot. This increases the total file size eight-fold. And that's just for the image portion of the page. Text and other graphic elements would add even more to the file size.

This is something of a worst-case scenario, because you would rarely want to scan a gray-scale image at 300 dpi. But even at 100 or 150 dpi, a gray-scale image in a PostScript file can quickly eat up your disk.

A standard PostScript file can contain several pages. But because of this tendency to eat up disk space, you may want to produce your PostScript files one page at a time. Another way to reduce disk space is to use a file compression program such as Stuff-It, which reduces the size of PostScript files by as much as 60 percent.

File Transfer

PostScript files can be transported by several means. Service bureau users generally transmit them over phone lines by means of a modem. They can also be transported via diskette. These can be the 1.2 megabyte diskettes used in AT and 386 computers, or the 1.44 megabyte or 800K diskettes used on the Macintosh. Iomega's Bernoulli Box uses removable 20- and 40-megabyte hard disks that can be used to transport PostScript files to a service bureau. The problem here is that the service bureau and client must both have compatible disk drive units.

File Structure

Unless your PostScript file is in EPSF format, you can open it with a word processor or text editor and see the commands used to produce the page. These commands conform to a strict structure specified by Adobe Systems in its programming guides. If the structure is altered, or if any mistakes are made in the programming code, the page will be printed incorrectly or not at all.

Header

All PostScript files begin with a "header" that provides essential information about its origin and contents. Some of this information must be present for the file to be printed. Other commands are optional. Header information can include a title, the date and time the file was created, the version of PostScript used to create it, and the author of the program. If the PostScript file was created by a software package like Adobe Illustrator, the program is listed as the author. Another important piece of information is the bounding box. This is a set of numbers that indicate the overall dimensions of the page. Header comments are always preceded by two percentage signs: %%. The %%EndComments command indicates the end of the header information.

Imaging Commands

After the header come the commands that produce the actual image. This book makes no pretense to being a PostScript programming manual; several good ones are available. But as you can see, it consists of commands and numeric coordinates that describe how an image is to be constructed. Some of the commands may seem cryptic, but in many cases they are spelling out a relatively simple operation. For example, the commands to draw a square would amount to saying: "Go north 12 paces, then west 12 paces, then south 12 paces, then east 12 paces." Another command might instruct the program to fill the square with a 10-percent gray shade.

Fonts

Any PostScript file that contains text must include information about the fonts used in the document. Fonts can be included as part of the PostScript file. If not, the file must include a command that downloads any fonts that are not resident in the output device. In many cases, a program that produces a PostScript file will include references to all fonts in the system, not just those used in that particular document.

One of the most important commands in any PostScript file is the *showpage* operator. After the instructions to construct the page are processed, the *showpage* command tells the RIP to go ahead and produce the page on the printer or imagesetter. If the *showpage* command has been deleted from a PostScript file, it will be unable to produce a page.

Producing PostScript Files

Each program has its own method for producing PostScript files. This is true even on the Macintosh, which is often distinguished by its consistency in implementing common functions across different programs. It is especially true in the IBM-compatible environment, which has always been characterized by a certain degree of anarchy in the way various software packages handle their printing functions.

Programs generally produce PostScript files in one of three ways: through the printing function, the file save function, or a file export function. In most cases, the latter two functions are used by graphics packages to create EPSF files for exchange with other programs. Adobe Illustrator, for example, saves files in EPSF as its native format. Corel Draw, a popular IBM drawing package, uses a file export function to create EPSF files. These EPSF files can be used to print pages and exchange graphic images with other software packages. As an output format, EPSF files differ from standard PostScript files in just one respect: while PostScript files can contain a range of pages, EPSF files can produce just one page at a time.

Most publishing programs, including Aldus PageMaker and Xerox Ventura Publisher, produce PostScript files as part of the printing function (Figure 4-5). You give the Print command, but instead of printing to an actual output

Figure 4-5.
PageMaker allows you
to print a PostScript file
to disk using the Print
dialog box.

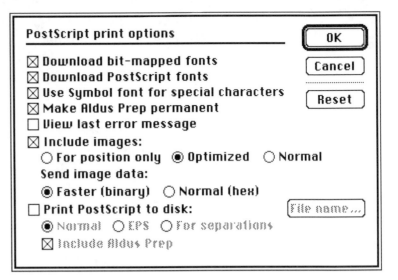

device, you print to a PostScript file. Some graphics programs can also create PostScript files in this manner. Corel Draw, for example, allows you to print a PostScript file to disk in addition to creating EPSF files. Unlike the EPSF files created by Corel Draw, these "print to disk files" cannot be used to import an image into another program. Don't assume, however, that any graphics package that prints to disk can automatically create a PostScript file. GEM Artline, for example, produces PostScript files by means of an explicit PostScript command. The program's print to disk function produces a disk file that is not compatible with PostScript devices.

In most packages, "Print to disk" is an option when you give the Print command. For example, when you open the Print dialog box in Aldus PageMaker, an Options button opens a second dialog box that allows you to specify that the document be produced as a PostScript disk file. When you choose this option, you are prompted to enter a file name, after which the program generates the appropriate PostScript file.

Ventura Publisher uses a somewhat different approach. Here, the "Print to Disk" option is found in the Set Printer

Info dialog box under the Options menu. After selecting "PostScript" as your output device, you can choose from a number of interface ports that the printer can be connected to: LPT1: and LPT2: for parallel connections, or COM1: or COM2: for serial connections. The last "port" listed is "Filename." When you select this, the program is set up to print any documents in the form of a PostScript disk file. When you give the Print command, the program prompts you for the name of the file you want to create and produces it. Its default file extension for PostScript files is "C00," but you can change this if you want.

Font Management

One important consideration when producing a PostScript file for output is font management. If you try to print a document containing a certain typeface on a PostScript device that does not include that font, the printing software will substitute Courier. You must thus be sure that any fonts called for in your document are present in the output device. If not, the fonts must be included in the PostScript file or downloaded by means of a command in the PostScript file.

Most publishing packages handle this font downloading automatically. But in some cases, you may have to specify how fonts are to be handled. In Corel Draw, for example, users are provided with a set of fonts named after famous cities that are equivalent to the Adobe/Linotype fonts used in most PostScript output devices. Corel's Avalon font, for example, is equivalent to Adobe's Avant Garde. If you want to print a Corel Draw document on an imagesetter with Adobe/Linotype fonts, you need to check the "all fonts resident" option after you give the print command. When you do this, Corel Draw replaces its own typefaces with the equivalent Adobe fonts as it creates the PostScript file. But if the Adobe fonts are not present in the imagesetter, it will replace them with Courier. The alternative is to keep the Corel fonts in the document and manually download them to the imagesetter.

In addition to downloading fonts, a PostScript file created by a publishing or graphics package can include most of the same effects found on a printed page. Some packages allow you to produce multiple versions of a document as color separations or overlays. A color image generally consists of four components in varying intensities: cyan, yellow, magenta, and black. If your publishing or graphics package supports color separations, it will produce one PostScript file for each of the four color components. Some programs also allow you to enlarge or reduce the page as it is printed in the PostScript file. Corel Draw provides the ability to produce a reversed — negative—version of the page. This can be useful if you want to produce film negatives on an imagesetter.

Downloading PostScript Files

Once a PostScript file has been created, it can be produced on a laser printer or imagesetter by a process known as downloading. The file is copied to the PostScript RIP, which processes the PostScript commands as if you were printing directly from a publishing or graphics program.

Several methods are available for downloading PostScript files. If you have an IBM-compatible computer that is directly connected to the imagesetter, you can issue a simple DOS copy command. For example, if the imagesetter is connected to the first parallel port (commonly known as LPT1), the following command will download the file to the output device:

```
COPY FILE.PS LPT1:
```

If your computer is part of a LAN, you can use the network software to download the file. The TOPS network, for example, includes a printing utility called NETPRINT that allows you to download a PostScript file to any printer or imagesetter on the network. Once the software has been correctly configured, you simply type PRINT followed by the file name.

Macintosh users can download PostScript files by means of a downloading program. These programs are generally quite easy to use. First, you use the Macintosh system Chooser to select the printer or imagesetter on which you want to produce the file. Then you simply choose the downloading option and double-click on the name of the file you want to print.

PostScript Level 2

With the advent of PostScript Level 2, Adobe has built on the foundation of the original PostScript language and tied together products used only in some PostScript products such as color printers, Japanese-language printers, and Display PostScript systems.

Some of the features of PostScript Level 2 that were not previously available include support for JPEG compressed images, support for different color spaces, and support for CCITT Group 3 facsimile images.

Using Desktop Publishing as an Advertising Tool

APPLICATION BRIEF

Barry Haynes wanted to demonstrate what could be done with the Macintosh desktop color environment, so he created "The Growing Revolution in Desktop Color," an eight-page glossy brochure. The images were scanned from 35mm film with a Nikon scanner, then color corrected with Adobe Photoshop or ColorStudio. The color separations were generated from ColorStudio, the duotones were printed from Photoshop, and the type and layout done in PageMaker 4.0. A diagram in the book was done with Freehand 2.0.

The bottom line was that this showed the high quality potential of color desktop publishing and helped people understand what they might get from the world of digital color photography.

Putting Four-Color Images on the Page

When it comes to putting four-color images on a page, you get into the critical geometry of building pages. Newsletters and magazines are easy since they have a consistent grid. The problem is with four-color ads that have fancy typography as well as color. You have the classic problems of typography and of color control interacting with each other. Even if you solve it on screen, it may not come out of the the imagesetter or film recorder. All the careful work on the computer does no good at all unless you can get the output.

An example is a project in which a company processed an ad for a client. It was a single page with five photographs on it, some type, reverses, and color type. The page had a gradient background running from a teal blue dark at the top to zero at the bottom. If it had been done conventionally using duplicate transparencies and films, this page would have required a good three days worth of work.

The work was handed in by the client on a 3 1/2-inch disk accompanied by a black-and-white copy print. In their effort to produce the page wanted by the client, the company ran into the classic problem encountered by service bureaus. The client had only taken a day to produce it and he expected the processing organization to take only a day or less to output it.

The problems began to mount up quickly. None of the windows left in that file had representational art. Identification was not provided for the transparencies, which were done as EPS files, but nowhere was there a naming convention of the photographs. The people using the new electronic form did not know how to provide art work in the conventional way, which should have been labeled sand percentages given. At least photostats of the photographs should have been provided for reference.

In the transition between conventional and electronic, there are a significant number of people building color pages of type and photographs who do not have much or any experience in conventional page layout. As a result, they may send in an EPS file with a gradient over an 8 1/2 or an 11-inch page going from a zero dot to a combination color with a maximum of 256 gradations. They expect a smooth gradient, but instead will get bands because they can assign only 256 gray levels. You can't get subtlety in the gradient without having many more gray levels.

One of the things that people who are producing electronic page design on a daily basis need to know is how files are handled by the output device. How the output device puts dots down is critical to the designer. Round dots are traditional and require good registration. Elliptical dots tolerate a little bit of overlap and they are not as critical in registration. They are more forgiving on press. In fashion advertising, elliptical dots are used for softer focus and better color rendering.

We refer to PostScript as being a *de facto* standard. In reality, the page designer has to establish a working relationship with a tremendous body of knowledge in order to know what to send.

Compressing Stock Photographs

APPLICATION BRIEF

Comstock, one of the nation's largest stock photography agencies, uses Kodak ColorSqueeze Image Compression Software to compress digital color image files for efficient transmission from the New York City headquarters to customers' Macintosh computers. Publishers link their Macintosh computers with Comstock's system and download a specific page with 72-dot-per-inch resolution suitable for layouts and composite pages. Duplicate transparencies are sent by overnight express delivery.

File Handling

After you have made the pages to your satisfaction on the screen, you now have to hand over your images and type to your output device. The way your files are handled is critical.

There are radically different ways in which the files are handled. One way is to envision that you are looking at your screen through different layers—one layer for type, another layer for page geometry, and so on. In the page geometry layer are all the addresses and X-Y coordinates, dimensions, and rotations for all the photos. You have dot-for-dot X-Y coordinates of the starting points relative to that box or that window where you bring in all your PICT, EPS, or TIFF files.

If your type has a transparent background, the software must address the question whether it is a transparent background over a white or a transparent background over a continuous tone or a tint. And if over color, should it be knocked out of all four colors? Should it carry an outline around the type that will trap to a tint? Or should it back off from a tint?

These situations are handled radically different depending on what tint you are going into. A lot of this is just trial and error.

Visionary has a whole layer of picture information that you can get to as a user, and it gives you addressing down to the fourth decimal place in millimeters. Most people doing the craft or the creative work don't want to get into that, but it is there. That's part of the advantage of the technology—it carries that baggage for you.

Selecting People for Page Layout

In the old film-based method of page layout, the page designer would simply draw in the rules where he wanted the page elements to be placed and a skilled craftsman in a service bureau would take care of placing the elements.

Today the person at the screen also has to be that skilled craftsman. He or she has to be able to place the image exactly on the page where it is to be printed. That is why layout guidelines are so important.

You can bring in a guideline and then snap your rules to the guideline. If the person doing page design doesn't take a regimented procedural approach, he or she will end up with something that does not look quite right. What you'll see is drifting windows, color with a halo around it, and four-color that has a white gap up against a rule.

The unfortunate thing is that many people will assume that it is the technology that can't handle it. We blame the tool instead of the technician, when in fact the tool can handle the problem if it is used correctly. What it will take is experience, understanding, and feedback from the person who outputs the work of the technician or designer.

Electronic Images from the Super Bowl

**APPLICATION
BRIEF**

Color and black-and-white Super Bowl photos were transmitted in under three minutes per transmission. Using Nikon scanners and compression system, images were compressed to 1/40th of their size in seconds using standard JPEG baseline methods. Pictures reached such publications as the New York Times, Newsday , Miami Herald, and 18 other newspapers via Knight Ridder's Electronic Bulletin Board, PressLink.

The Test Page

The only way to do it right is to set up a test page and run it to a vendor who will provide the feedback for you. As one person observed, "This is a dance and we're not sure who is leading, what the tempo is, and certainly what's the expertise of the dancers."

Since most users of page make-up software will be using outside services for output, it may require a great deal of time before both parties are comfortable with the results. If users select a vendor who is willing to work with them, they are way ahead of the game.

People who have recently entered the service bureau business recognize that they have to spend time training the artists who are bringing the work to them. How do you charge somebody for this? The artist wants to bring work in and wants the vendor to do it. Why should the artist go through two or three days of training prior to giving work to the vendor? Why should the vendor fund that training? The real answer is self-preservation. Both the user and the vendor doing the output will lose. No vendor wants to get work that they will not be able to process.

Everybody has heard the horror stories of trying to output an EPS file and after an hour the machine has not budged. We can compare this to the relationship of printing images and type in black-and-white at 300 dpi or 1200 dpi. When you output a page from an application at 300 it takes half an hour, maybe 45 minutes; when you output that at 1200 dpi , it is not just a linear relationship of four times as long, it reaches the physical capacity of the amount of memory in the machine. When there is no work-around internally, there is no way for PostScript to know that it can't handle it. PostScript continues to try to process it. After an hour and a half with nothing coming out of the 1200 dpi machine, you finally cancel the request for print.

There are all sorts of horror stories related by service bureaus. They take in a page that looks relatively simple, but the way the EPS files are created, overlapped, and generally put together, the job takes an hour to print when it should have taken ten minutes. It has to be charged at an hourly rate.

E.s.p.r.i.t. Is a Labor of Love

**APPLICATION
BRIEF**

Students at the Rochester Institute of Technology put out a full-color magazine that is produced using electronic photography and computers. No conventional or mechanical typesetting, stripping, page composition, or color separations are used. All aspects of RIT's E.s.p.r.i.t. are electronic, from photography and design to prepress production. Analog and digital still cameras, as well as scanned images, are combined in Macintosh computers and separations are produced electronically.

E.s.p.r.i.t. is the title of the publication and the initials stand for Electronic Still Photography at Rochester Institute of Technology. Since its first issue in May 1989, E.s.p.r.i.t. has been a showcase for electronic still photography by students. E.s.p.r.i.t. continues today as a volunteer project, but it is more than that, it is a unique opportunity for both students and faculty to learn about electronic still photography.

When first produced, the students had to work with limited hardware and software. Today, with support from more than a dozen companies, the students have a variety of software, cameras, and scanners. Final page layouts are stored on SyQuest 44-megabyte removable hard disks, which are then taken to campus sites that have PostScript imagesetters. E.s.p.r.i.t. is a testing ground for visual ideas and technical solutions and is the work of volunteer student editors under the direction of Professor Douglas Ford Rea.

Black-and-White and Duotone Images

With black-and-white and duotones (using two inks to produce a monochrome print with more gradation), you have the same problems in highlight, mid-tone, and shadow detail that you run into in four-color work. The images being represented on the screen become even more deceptive when you try to make a black-and-white image on a color monitor. Higher resolution screens will help because then you can address more pixels and create more levels of gray in the screen image.

The best that you can do on most screens is 72 dpi. That is less than what your eye can normally see on film or prints. What do you use for judgment on the monitor? How do you control the image and type with that resolution?

One answer might be to use the concept of four-stop photography. The four-stop photography concept as it is applied to film says you are using the best dynamic range that you can expect when you print the final image. We don't apply this to black-and-white. What should you expose for in black-and-white? Usually, just a nice gray tone with some detail in the shadow. You are going to want to carry detail in dots even in the highlight, otherwise you are going to have a printing nightmare.

The question is how do you prevent that potential nightmare? If you have calibrated something for color, consider that you have to throw away information to calibrate it for black-and-white. You must preserve detail and not have it blossom in the highlight areas. Blossoming is a term not used in black-and-white photography, but it certainly is in video. Pure white is all you've got there.

Because of the limited dynamic range of a video camera, there may be problems with highlights. You often lose detail in shadow areas because of saturation.

Covering the Bush-Gorbachev Summit for Time Magazine

APPLICATION BRIEF

To meet a deadline, pictures shot by Time photographers at summit sites in Malta were flown to a photolab in Rome. The developed film was scanned in minutes by a Nikon portable direct film scanner and transmitted in low resolution for preview purposes to Time's New York City offices in 20 minutes.

Once the editors in New York selected pictures, high-resolution images were transmitted on the Crosfield system while two others were rescanned on the Nikon scanner and transmitted to New York. Final forms were transmitted to Time's various printing plants to meet deadlines for the issue to reach readers on Monday morning.

Part of the overall success was a new portable multi-tasking electronic imaging system designed by National Digital Corporation for Time.

Fonts

Desktop publishers hear the terms "font" and "typeface" used interchangeably, but it was not always so. In the pre-PostScript typesetting era, the term "typeface" referred to a specific design of type, such as Times Roman or Helvetica Bold. "Typeface family" referred to a group of typefaces installed as a unit, such as "Times Roman, Times Bold, Times Italic and Times Bold Italic." "Font" referred to a specific typeface in a specific size, such as "14-point Times Bold."

These distinctions made sense at the time. In older typesetting systems, fonts were loaded in distinct sizes and styles.

A typesetter equipped with 14-, 18-, 24-, and 36-point Times Bold, for example, would be unable to produce a headline in 30-point Times bold unless you added that font.

In contrast, desktop publishing systems use "scalable fonts." Instead of loading fonts in distinct sizes, you load one copy of each typeface, such as Times and Helvetica in normal, bold, italic, and bold-italic styles. When you specify a type size in a desktop publishing program and print the document, the PostScript software enlarges the typeface to the desired size.

This is why the meaning of "font" has changed. To a PostScript user who can scale type to almost any size, "font" generally refers to a typeface or even an entire typeface family. "Typeface" generally refers to the design of the type. You don't hear people say, "I just installed 14- and 18-point Broadway." Instead, they've installed a copy of the Broadway display face that can be enlarged from four to 1000 points and any size in between (depending on the capabilities of your software).

As we have seen, these sizes are stated in "points," the unit long used in the print production business to measure type size. One point is equal to approximately one-seventy-second of an inch. The "point size" of a font is the maximum amount of space required for characters. For example, if you set the word "High Jump" in 72-point Helvetica, it will measure about 1 inch from the top of the "H" to the bottom of the "p."

Typeface Characteristics

Typeface design is an age-old art form that dates to the times of Gutenberg. Type designers say that creating a new typeface is an artistic achievement on the level of a novel or a symphony. Each typeface has unique characteristics, and usually represents many long hours of design work even with the computer-aided design software available today.

Typographers use a rather large vocabulary to describe the shapes of characters. An ascender is the portion of certain lowercase characters—b, d, f, h, k, l, t—that rises above the main body of the character. A descender is the portion of other lower-case characters—g, j, p, q, y—that descend below the baseline. "X-height" is the main body of a character measured from the baseline, without ascenders or descenders. If you look through a type catalog, you'll notice that some fonts have larger x-heights than others. In addition to ascenders and descenders, type designers use terms like "stem," "link," and "bowl" to describes the sections of a character shape.

Serifs
One feature that immediately distinguishes one font from another is the presence or absence of serifs—tiny crossbars used on the ends of character shapes. Typefaces with serifs are often used for body text in newspapers, books, and magazines because many people regard them as being easy to read. Typefaces without serifs—sans serif typefaces— are often used in headlines. The most well known serif typeface is probably "Times," while the most well known sans serif typeface is "Helvetica."

The way serifs are designed in a particular typeface often provide its special look. Optima, for example, has small, barely noticeable serifs. Garamond has rounded, triangular serifs. Lubalin Graph has large, squared-off serifs. Other features that distinguish one typeface from another include its character width, the amount of difference between thick and thin lines, and a factor known as stress, which refers to the degree of slant in the main body of the character.

Font Variations

Most typefaces are created in four to six variations. The "plain" or "roman" style is the basic version of the typeface intended for use as body text. "Italic" refers to a slanted design used in body text for titles and emphasis. Sometimes the term "oblique" is used to describe roman character designs that are slanted by the software rather than being designed from scratch. "Bold" refers to a thick, heavy version of the typeface, used in headlines and also for emphasis in body text. "Bold italic" combines the bold and italic styles. Some typefaces also come in condensed and expanded variations. Others come in a "light" version slightly thinner than the roman weight, or a "demibold" version slightly thicker than roman but thinner than bold. Some typefaces can be printed in "outline" or "shadow" formats. Instead of being installed as separate fonts, these styles are created from the outlines of existing fonts. Some decorative and script typefaces, such as Cooper Black, Dom Casual, and Park Avenue, are available in one or two weights only.

Another factor that distinguishes typefaces is proportional versus monospaced character spacing. In most typefaces, characters occupy varying amounts of space depending on their size. An "I," for example, occupies less space than an "M." This is known as "proportional spacing." In a monospaced typeface, each character occupies a fixed amount of space no matter what its size. Proportional typefaces are generally preferred because they are easy to read and economize on space. But monospaced fonts are sometimes used for certain effects, such as imitating the output of a typewriter. The popular Courier typeface, for example, is a monospaced font designed for this very purpose.

Character Sets

One more distinction among fonts is the character sets they include. Almost every font includes the standard alphabet in upper- and lower-case plus numerals and the symbols commonly found on a typewriter. Most typefaces also include additional symbols found in what's known as the standard ASCII character set. To produce one of these symbols, you type an ASCII code or a combination of keys, depending on your hardware and software. For example, you can enter a bullet symbol (•) on a Macintosh by typing an "8" while you hold down the Option key.

Some specialty typefaces include non-English language character sets or symbol collections. One of the most popular symbol typefaces is Zapf Dingbats, which includes snowflakes, check marks and other symbols. Each symbol is linked to a standard key on the keyboard. When you type an "A" in Zapf Dingbats, you get a Star of David (✡).

There is the legal question of font licensing. Service bureaus are handing the fonts back and forth to the clients, and clients are taking their licensed fonts and are passing it to the service bureau just so they can output it. The service bureau needs the font from the screen as well as the printer font—they're necessary for processing the file. If at the last minute for some reason the page has to be opened, to see it on the screen, you must have the screen font. Some licenses allow this type of font movement as long as the font is used only to produce a document for the licensed user. Some type vendors have licensed fonts that can travel with the document. Once created, anyone can make a copy of the document file and use it to print out the document with the licensed font.

Learning the System Needs

The digital photographer who is going to be in four color publishing has a lot more to worry about than just getting through image enhancement and page layout systems.

In putting digital images and type together, you must be aware of file size, fonts, spreads and chokes, and other things we have discussed. You have to know what files you must put in the folder to send to the output service so they can produce the equivalent of what you saw on the screen.

Two out of three files will not work, four out of five will not work. If you created five files for the document, they all have to be sent.

Finally, test it, and not in the eleventh hour. Do your testing before you start production and have somebody knowledgeable enough to know what the results of the tests mean.

It's very easy to have something in the file that you cannot see on the screen and yet when it gets to the output device, the output device is going to try to output it.

Middle East Photo Coverage by Electronics

Time, Newsweek, and U.S. News and World Report used National Digital Corporation high-resolution transmission systems to transmit magazine quality photos from Saudi Arabia using standard phone lines.

APPLICATION BRIEF

CHAPTER 5

Proofing and Printing Digital Photographs

With all of the enhancement, page make-up, and modification of digital photographs you might possibly do, you must be able to view an accurate copy of what you have done. Soft proofing can be done on a calibrated color monitor or LCD screens. Hard copies on film or paper can be produced on a wide variety of output devices. Hard copies on film can be reproduction-quality positives or negatives for platemaking, 35mm slides and larger transparencies. The output choices for paper are even greater, ranging from inkjet or sublimation-dye color proofs to bright and inexpensive thermal-wax prints.

Soft Proofing of Digital Photo Images

The most practical means of viewing digital photo images directly from the computer is the use of the CRT (cathode ray tube). The CRT workhorse is over 100 years old and only recently has there been any move to other display technologies.

Liquid crystal display (LCD) screens are found in most laptop computers. Color LCDs are beginning to appear, but so far they have limited resolution capabilities. Projection LCD systems show greater promise since it is possible to create dichroic filters that would be more precisely matched to color photographic printing or to the inks used on printing presses—more so than the phosphors of CRT systems.

Other flat panel technology includes plasma displays, light emitting diode (LED) displays and electroluminescent (EL) panels.

CRT Monitors

A CRT is basically a glass tube that is sealed and contains an electronic gun for generating a electron beam, a deflection yoke for focusing the electronic beam, and a phosphor-coated screen that glows when it is struck by the electron beam. With color screens, a single pixel is composed of three phosphor dots, red, blue, and green, which are struck by the electron beam through a screen or mask. Resolution of the CRT is a function of the size of the hole in the shadow mask through which the electron beam moves so it strikes the correct dot (Figure 5-1).

Figure 5-1. A cross-section sketch of a typical conventional color tube (left), and a Sony Trinitron color tube (right).

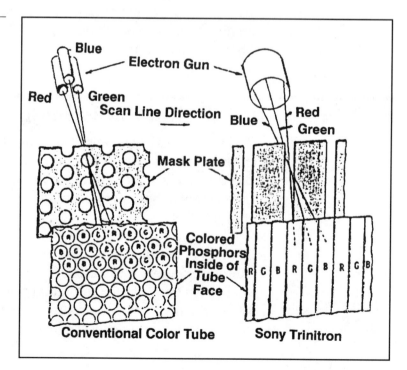

The rate at which data is sent to the monitor is referred to as bandwidth, with a higher resolution screen needing a higher bandwidth. Monitor quality will depend on screen resolution. The finer the pitch of the screen (the size of a single pixel), the sharper will be the image. As the scanned frequency increases, so does the information being sent to the screen.

Today's color monitors are available from standard EGA levels to a pixel level of 2048 by 2048 dots. The monitor you select still needs to match the display card in your computer. Anything beyond that would be wasteful because the cost increases dramatically as the size of the monitor increases modestly. The higher resolution monitors are found on application-specific systems which are designed for operation with the higher frequency signal. Multisynch monitors automatically adjust to the signal from the display board within the computer and are easier to install.

The quality of CRT color monitors is not standing still—it continues to improve in sharpness and resolution. The main limitation of the CRT is found in the phosphors. Considerations like persistence (how long the phosphors glow after a charge is removed) and brightness limit the phosphors we can use. Most of today's phosphors are designed to meet the needs of the home television set. This is a good standard but does not meet the needs of the digital photographer or desktop publisher.

Prototype color monitors displayed by companies such as Sony maintain a stable color purity within plus or minus 1 percent over 500 hours for black-and-white balance levels. A recent prototype Sony unit uses a current beam feedback system to ensure that the color temperature remains stabilized over a long period.

Internalized calibration is also used for color monitors. The Barco Calibrator has a self-contained microprocessor that enables the standard level to be checked on the screen. An accessory device can be added to adjust the brightness level of the monitor to compensate for the ambient room light.

Individual color calibrators are also appearing from several companies. RasterOps CorrectColor Calibrator uses four photocells to read the color monitor's white temperature and gamma value. Within a base unit, two microprocessors perform color correction calculations and can interconnect to a host computer.

The Radius Precision Color Calibrator not only checks the monitor but also lets the viewer compare Pantone color simulations for matching purposes.

More work continues on improving CRT technology. Zenith is developing larger forms of its 14-inch flat tension mask (FTM) for high resolution color display. The key advantage of the FTM is its greater brightness, increased contrast and the ability to hold colors better since there is less movement of the mask behind the screen. The perfectly flat screen also is a major benefit for illustrators and desktop publishers.

Development also goes on to develop a very thin, flat CRT. A number of companies both in the United States and Japan have actively worked on the flat CRT as an alternative to LCD screens. A Matsushita demonstration flat CRT used a beam-index system with a single electron gun and no shadow mask to create colors, while a U.S. company employed microscopic cathodes to create the individual colors.

LCD Screens

Some 25 years ago, a young researcher at RCA came up with an invention for a flat, lightweight video screen on which images can be formed by applying electric current to an organic material called a liquid crystal. The current flat-panel LCDs use "active matrix" thin-film transistor (TFT) technology, in which hundreds of thousands of transistors work as switching elements. TFTs make it possible to create a liquid crystal screen with a brightness, contrast, and refresh rate that was not possible before. Active matrix technology was a product of Westinghouse from some 20 years ago.

Several forms of LCD displays are available today. The twisted nematic, one of the earliest LCD devices, had two simple polarizing layers (Figure 5-2). The supertwist liquid crystal that was developed later rotates the plane of polarization between 180 and 270 degrees, as compared to the 90 degrees of the twisted nematic. The double-supertwist display includes a color-compensating cell.

Active-matrix is a complex technology, but has produced color displays of an acceptable quality for many data processing and graphic applications. The color can be boosted to provide even more subtle colors by the use of

Figure 5-2. How a twisted nematic LCD works.

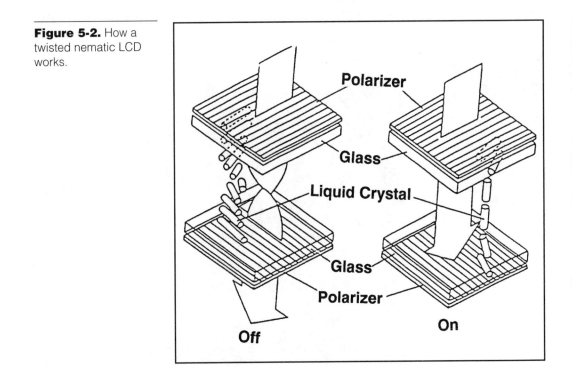

color LCD interface controllers. Instead of the usual red, green, and blue filters, In Focus Systems is developing a display that uses cyan, yellow, and magenta filters, which is the same subtractive method of producing full color used in printing.

The idea of a flat television screen that could be simply hung on a wall has been pursued for some time. Recently, Sharp Corp. began to market full-color LCD screens that are designed to be hung on the wall (Figure 5-3).

A new LCD panel developed by IBM and Toshiba provides a 720 by 550 pixel 16-color active matrix LCD. This may become one of the more popular screens for laptop computers in the future.

The development of LCD screens may be further enhanced by the introduction of ferroelectronic liquid-crystal displays. The advantage of the ferroelectronic screen is that it does not require the large number of transistors required by the LCD technology, which makes it an easier screen to manufacture.

Figure 5-3. Wall-mounted flat-screen television, once a science fiction fantasy, is now a reality. Sharp has developed full-color LCD units called the "Liquid Crystal Museum" and is marketing the series in Japan. (Courtesy Sharp Electronics Corp.)

Projection LCDs may also find their way into use in digital photography. Resolution improvements have appeared from companies such as Sharp and Greyhawk that allow resolutions approaching, or in some cases surpassing, the resolution of most high-end CRT monitors.

With projection liquid crystal systems, filters that match the dye characteristics of printing materials and printing presses can be constructed—something which has not been possible with CRT phosphors. That would open the way to accurate and "live" CYMK soft proofing.

Plasma Displays

In plasma displays, a gas mixture glows when an electrical current is generated at the intersection of two wires. The first plasma monitors, which were in 18- to 20-inch square sizes, emitted a red-orange glow using a standard neon gas mixture.

The technology has now advanced through the use of an ultraviolet-emitting xenon gas mixture. The UV is used to excite a photoluminescent phosphor, which produces a color image.

The latest displays demonstrated showed motion but still needed greater resolution than is currently available, but this can be expected in the near future.

Other Flat Panels

Light emitting diodes (LED) first served as signaling devices on control panels, but before long they appeared in high-speed copiers as a way of writing digital information in unique one LED per pixel form. Screens using numerous LEDs have been developed for advertising and commercial applications. This has been especially encouraged now with the development of a missing color for LEDs—a blue LED. Only recently has a blue LED made of silicon carbide appeared in the market.

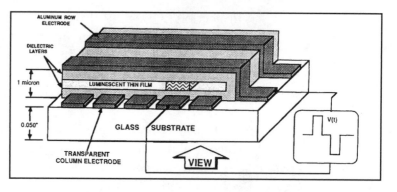

Figure 5-4. A cross-section of an electroluminescent panel display. (Courtesy Planar Corp.)

The display application of LEDs may be somewhat distant, but the LEDs as printing devices are finding their way into photo-quality printers and other devices.

Another technology that has been used for monochrome screens by Grid Computer is the electroluminescent (EL) panel display (Figure 5-4). The resolution of this display can be as high as 100 lines per inch with a viewing angle greater than 140 degrees. The EL glass panel is a solid-state device with a thin-film luminescent layer sandwiched between transparent dielectric layers. The row electrodes in back are aluminum and the column electrodes in front are transparent. The column and active electrodes are arranged in vertical and horizontal rows forming intersecting pixels.

Much work has been done to develop an electroluminescent color display and the first samples have been shown for this form of technology.

Photo Shops Offer Still Video Prints

APPLICATION BRIEF

Making prints from analog still-video cameras is a new service that can be provided by photo shops to customers. Using thermal-dye transfer printers, the 275 stores of Ritz Camera have begun to make color prints from their customers' still-video camera images.

Color Prints from Digital Photographs

Most of the printers used for making color prints from digital photographs perform the function with three colors. Usually these colors are cyan, magenta, and yellow (CYM). There are also color printers that match the full CYMK (K for black) process (Figure 5-5).

Between the printer and computer, you will usually find a raster image processor (RIP) or a page description language (PDL). This, either software or software/hardware solution, allows the passage of information to the printing device so the printing device knows where to place the image on paper. The price of the printer selected will have some degree of relationship to the quality of the image.

Figure 5-5. A wide variety of technologies are used to put digital images onto paper or film.

Hard Copy Options

Type	Black-and-White	Color
Thermal		
Direct (Leuco Dye)	X	
Dye Transfer	X	X
Wax		X
Electrophotographic		
Laser	X	X
LED	X	X
Inkjet		
Continuous Stream		X
Drop-on-Demand	X	X
Conventional Photo Film and Paper (Silver Halide)		
Drum Scanner	X	X
Dry Silver	X	X
Film Camera	X	X
Laser		X
LCD		X
Light Valve (PLZT)	X	X
Pictrography		X

While this is changing today with better quality appearing with lower prices, it is still not possible to produce a high quality print on a very inexpensive printer.

Some color printers can create photorealistic color images from digital photographs. Photorealistic prints do not meet the same requirements that a screened separation color proof does. A proof made from the separation negatives is called a contract proof in the printing industry. Entire systems have been developed to provide contract proofs to printing customers.

Thermal-Dye Transfer

Thermal-dye transfer is often called dye sublimation or dye-diffusion thermal-transfer (D2T2). Whatever name is used, the process uses a gravure-printed dye sheet and a thermal head. The thermal head transfers energy through the dye sheet to a photography-type paper or transparency material (Figure 5-6).

The resolution of the thermal-dye transfer printers range from 160 to 300 dpi, with print sizes from 3 1/2 by 5 inches to 14 by 17 inches. Resolution is limited by the very nature of the thermal printing head.

The quality of a thermal-dye transfer print from most printers strongly resembles the print from conventional silver halide color or black-and-white paper. The maxi-

Figure 5-6. In thermal-dye transfer printing, a variable-heat head is used to transfer the colored ink from a film to the paper. The size of the ink dot that is transferred can be varied.

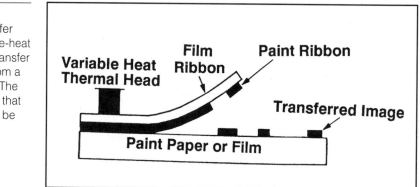

Figure 5-8. Hitachi VY200A video printer produces snapshot-size color prints. (Courtesy Hitachi America Ltd.)

mum density can reach a level of 2.6 while the minimum density is very white at value of .05 log density units (Color Figure C5-7).

The cyan, yellow, and magenta dyes are individually written to the receiver. Occasionally thermal-dye transfer prints will show a streaking in a smooth gray or sky-colored area and this is due to either variability in the thermal head performance or movement of the paper, since the paper may not be held in perfect register as it passes through the three separate steps.

A variety of small 3 1/2 to 5 by 7 inch printers are available from Canon, Eastman Kodak, Fuji, Hitachi, NEC, Nikon, Panasonic, Sakura, Sharp, and Sony (Figure 5-8). Print time for most of these printers is 2 to 3 minutes. Many of the printers accept both RGB and video signal input, and some even have the ability to print freeze frames.

Printers for 8 by 10 or 11 by 11 inch format prints are available using thermal-dye transfer printers manufactured by Eastman Kodak, Hitachi, Gold Star, Mitsubishi, Seiko Instrument, and Sony (Figures 5-9 and 5-10). The largest D2T2 printer is the 4Cast Printer offered by DuPont. It produces a thermal-dye transfer print of 11.9 by 17.3 inches for the final image.

One unusual printer comes from Laser Technics. The Starburst dual-mode color printer will print on both thermal-dye transfer and thermal-wax material, with prints up to A4 in size. It takes three minutes for a full color thermal-dye transfer print and one minute for a thermal-wax print.

Inkjet Printers

Inkjet printers are not new. A simple form of inkjet printer has been used for many years for addressing mail at high-speeds. Early efforts by such companies as Canon to use

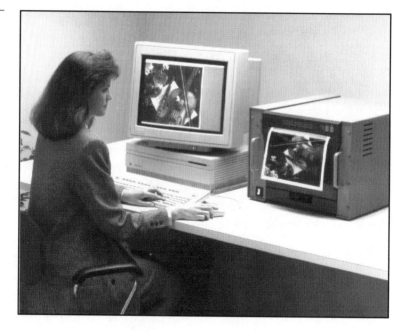

Figure 5-9. The Kodak XL 7700 digital continuous tone printer is a desktop unit that produces page-size pictures. (Courtesy Eastman Kodak)

inkjet for color was less than successful because of the inability to produce a long scale of color and sufficient color saturation to create a photorealistic image.

Today that problem has been overcome, first by Iris Graphics and subsequently by others. Iris, a Scitex company, has produced one of the highest quality digital printers by using a precisely controlled variable size dot of ink. While the actual addressable resolution of the Iris printer is 300 dots per inch, the perceived resolution is between 1500 to 1800 dpi. In addition, the Iris printer is able to print on a variety of media which makes it adaptable to a wide range of production situations from newsprint to transparent or translucent receiver material. The Iris inkjet is widely used by newspapers and service bureaus for color proofing.

Figure 5-10. The Sony digital color printer produces an A4-size thermal-dye transfer color print in less than two minutes. (Courtesy Sony Corporation of America)

The Stork inkjet uses the same technology as Iris does, but Stork developed their version independently and has developed a high quality inkjet printer. A thin stream of cyan, magenta, yellow or black ink is modulated to produce 625,000 droplets per second. The droplets are electrically

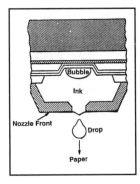

Figure 5-11. A cross-section of a bubble-jet nozzle.

charged according to information extracted from the image-data stream, and the charged droplets are deflected in flight by an electrical field. The uncharged droplets fly on and reach the substrate. The Stork inkjet prints at the rate of one inch per minute.

The Canon bubble-jet technology (Figure 5-11) was first applied in a copier designed to copy and enlarge photographs and artwork. Enlargements could be up to 1200 percent, and a 22 by 33-inch print took 6 minutes. Now digital interfaces have been provided making it possible to write digital photographs directly to paper or translucent receivers with a 400 dpi print level and 64 gradations per color.

There have been a number of other lower cost inkjet printers which are based on "drop-on-demand" technology. With these printers, ink is pumped only on command when necessary to place a point on paper. Canon, Hewlett-Packard, Kodak, and Tektronix have produced popular low-end color inkjet printers. HP's PaintJet and color Deskjets have brought the price of a desktop color printer below $1000.

Another version of inkjet is the solid inkjet which first appeared from Howtek. A wax-like crayon is melted and the wax acts just like the "drop-on-demand" and produces a color dot when called for by the digital information.

New versions of the solid inkjet are now appearing from Tektronix with their phase-change inkjet technology. The special inks for this process are solid at room temperature, then melted and sprayed onto the paper where they resolidify quickly with the color remaining on top of the paper instead of diffusing into the fibers of the paper. The result is a brighter color.

The phase-change inkjet printer uses piezoelectric crystals that vibrate to act as pumps driving the ink droplets from the printhead. Tek's PhaserJet, with its tabloid-size output, proved to be an instant hit with service bureaus looking for a PostScript color proofer for less than $10,000.

Copiers Are Now Electronic Color Printers

When color copiers first appeared, they basically served as pure copy devices, with the added capability of copying a slide by direct projection (Figure 5-12).

Today a number of different copiers are available that can be directly connected to a computer and accept digital signals for pages and photographs. These printers produce images with a true photorealistic look, with the exception of the fact that they are on plain, bond paper stock in most cases.

The Canon Color Laser Copier 500 has been one of the most popular of this new generation of printers. Many software

Figure 5-12.
Operation of a typical laser writing engine.

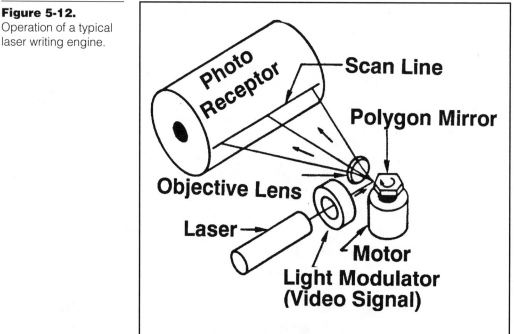

Figure 5-13. The Canon Color Laser Copier 500 can output directly from digital files on a computer as well as copy pages and film images. (Courtesy Canon USA)

packages have drivers to connect to the CLC 500. The addition of the PostScript-intelligent processing unit (PS-IPU) speeds up the processing (Figure 5-13).

The Colorocs color printer uses a straight-through paper path and can print up to 11 by 17-inch documents.

The Xerox Digital Color Copier can be connected to an PC or Macintosh and accept data directly. A future interface will allow the copier to accept data directly from a computer via an Adobe PostScript controller (Figure 5-14).

Digital Images Printed on Silver-Halide Media

Silver halide film and paper are used in several printers for creating images from digital photographs. The Fujix Pictrography 1000 uses a silver-halide photo-sensitive donor film and a plain receiving sheet. The donor is moistened and pressed against the receiver and the image is transferred thermally. The Pictrography 2000 added some significant technological changes. One of Fujix's major achievements was the development of a transfer compound that released color material when there is the transfer of a single electron. In addition, new developing agents and silver halide emulsion technology were created. Thermal development of 15 seconds produces quality color images (Figure 5-15). The printer used for Pictrography 2000 is an LED printer with the capability of printing at 284 dpi.

Figure 5-14. The Xerox 5775 Digital Color Copier produces 7 1/2 copies per minute. (Courtesy Xerox Corp.)

Another approach to digital photo imaging is from Ilford. The Ilford Digital Photo Imager produces continuous tone prints, overhead transparencies, and 35mm film from digital data. The signals are written by a laser onto three liquid crystal light valves (LCLV). The LCLV image is then projected onto the photographic media and processed.

The 3M Color Laser Imager writes on infrared color-sensitized paper. The lightbeams from the three laser

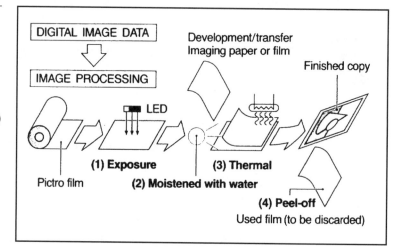

Figure 5-15. The Fujix Pictrography process is a new technology that uses a silver-halide film and thermal transfer to a receiving paper sheet. (Courtesy Texnai Corp.)

DIGITAL IMAGE DATA

IMAGE PROCESSING

Development/transfer Imaging paper or film

Finished copy

LED

Pictro film

(1) Exposure

(2) Moistened with water

(3) Thermal

(4) Peel-off

Used film (to be discarded)

diodes are combined into a single beam for writing on the paper. The printer has 256 addressable levels for each color and a resolution of 300 dpi.

Polaroid also turned to laser diodes for its Digital Image Printer, which uses Spectra Instant Print film. Less than 30 seconds is required to print a standard size Spectra print at 256 dpi horizontal and 165 dpi vertical at 8-bits per color.

Agfa has a digital print system for scanning 35mm slides, and then processing and outputting them to conventional photographic paper. Experiments with this system, which uses a CRT writer to image the standard color negative paper, showed that other digital photo images could be written using this system.

Light Valve Technology (LVT), a Kodak company, uses PLZT (lead lanthanum zirconate titanate) linear modulators as electro-optic modulating devices with a proprietary exposure system. Contrast ratios are greater than 1500 to 1, which gives good shadow detail (Figure 5-16). Modulation, triggered by voltage variations, controls the intensity of red, green, and blue light from three tungsten halogen lamps. With this system, resolutions on different models are 48 lines per millimeter up to 60 lines per millimeter.

Figure 5-16. The Kodak LVT digital image recorder is used for high-resolution film recording. The LVT can be linked directly to scanners, computers, color printers, and optical storage devices. (Courtesy Eastman Kodak)

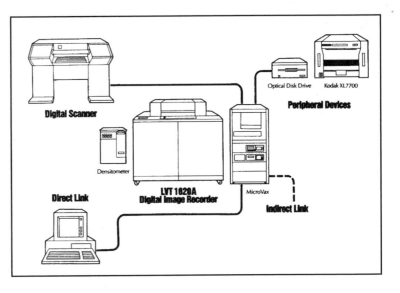

In addition to their lines of conventional color photographic materials and the special color paper for their laser printer, 3M has produced color and black-and-white dry silver products. These are photographic products that are exposed conventionally and produce color or black-and-white images with the application of heat to the silver emulsion. While dry silver products are not as stable as conventionally processed silver halide materials, they provide an opportunity for an instant look and printers have been developed to write digital information to dry silver color and black-and-white products.

In passing, there are at least two other forms of image recording materials which have appeared for digitally recording images. Direct thermal paper printers have been developed by Raytheon and Seikosha. The papers for these printers use a leuco dye that produces a monochrome-looking continuous tone image when digital images are written by a heat source.

Cycolor™ uses encapsulated color dye components. In one version of a digital printer that uses Cycolor technology, after being exposed to the image the donor material containing the encapsulated color particles is joined to a

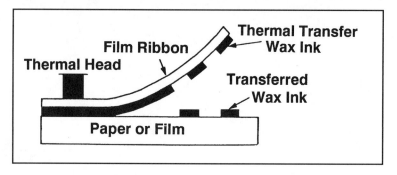

Figure 5-17. Thermal-wax printer uses a variable-heat head to transfer wax-based color from the film ribbon to the paper. Each point produced by the heat head is the same size.

receiver sheet, and both sheets passed through pressure rollers. A color image is released and transferred to the paper or transparent receiver.

Thermal-Wax-Transfer Printers

Thermal-wax-transfer printers, like most other color printers, are based on subtractive color and use cyan, magenta, and yellow to create a four-color image. The pigments subtract part of the spectrum of white light and the reflected light is seen by the viewer as color.

Thermal-wax printers are designed to produce clean, bright colors (Figure 5-17). This makes it difficult to use a thermal-wax print as a proof for offset printing because the colors are brighter than what can be done on the printing press. Also, the process colors used on the printing press produce a much wider range of colors than is possible on thermal-wax printers. Thermal-wax printers normally produce color only 1-bit per color deep and even with efforts to dither or modify the image, you still have only 1-bit per color in the final result.

The advantages of the thermal-wax printer are its low cost and ability to produce large prints relatively quickly.

Today a wide range of thermal-wax printers are available from companies such as Tektronix, Panasonic, Oce, QMS, and others (Figure 5-18).

Figure 5-18. Panasonic EPL-8543 Color Thermal Printer is an example of a desktop thermal-wax printer. (Courtesy Panasonic)

Film Cameras for Imaging

A number of cameras based on CRT technology are available today for recording images onto film, creating either a
transparency for viewing or a negative. These CRT imagers vary from very low-priced, low-resolution units for
35mm film up to units that record at 16,000 by 16,000
pixels on 8 by 10 film (Figure 5-19).

The original version of the CRT-based camera was developed for use in recording digital satellite images in the
1960s. Some of the lower priced film recorders were origi-

Figure 5-19. How a
typical film recorder
works. The image from
a monochrome CRT
passes through a color
wheel to a camera lens
and finally to the film.
Three or four separate
exposures are
required. (Courtesy
Afga Matrix)

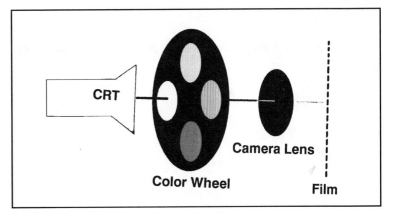

Figure 5-20. Letter formed by a film recorder with a CRT that has low addressability is jagged (left). When a recorder has a high addressability, the image is smooth (right). (Courtesy Agfa Matrix)

Figure 5-21. The Dicomed Captivator Film Recorder has a resolution of 16,000 lines per inch and is used to output high-resolution transparencies. (Courtesy Dicomed Inc.)

nally simple analog devices producing images that were only slightly better in resolution than the images from a standard home television screen (Figure 5-20).

The same technology, using black-and-white, high-resolution flat cathode-ray tubes, can produce very high resolution color images on film. Today the CRT-based cameras are digital and generally produce high-quality images. PostScript RIPs are available, for example, for Agfa Matrix Film Recorders.

The Dicomed Captivator Production Film Recorder includes resolution options from 2000 to 16,000 lines per inch for 35mm to 8 by 10-inch transparency films. Designed as a time-modulated device rather than intensity-modulated, the quality of the images is superior since the beam quality remains a constant (Figure 5-21).

The Solitaire Image Recorder from Management Graphics comes in a variety of models that can support up to 36 bits of total color. At 16,000 lines, an 8 by 10-inch photographic film can be exposed in as little as three minutes.

The digital Polaroid Palette is a good entry-level digital device, with a resolution of 2048 by 1366 pixels and addressable color of 8 bits per primary color.

Tektronix Provides Excellence in Color Centers

APPLICATION BRIEF

The Excellence in Color Center concept was pioneered by Tektronix to educate individual computer users in the effective use of color. Tektronix's goal is to help people understand how to use color and to increase productivity and effectiveness. Included in the centers is the Tektronix family of thermal and inkjet color printers.

Imagesetters for Color Separations

Imagesetters are the final step before printing plates are made. The imagesetter separates the digital color image and text files into its CYMK components. The CYMK separations for each page are printed on film, which then is used to make the plates for the press.

There are three types of imagesetters: flatbed, external drum, and internal drum. On flatbed imagesetters, the film is fed from a roll across a flatbed and the imaging head scans across the film as the film moves. These devices usually do not have register pins and there is difficulty in obtaining the registration quality.

External drum imagesetters are fed manually by a technician who places film on a drum and the drum rotates with the film held in place by a vacuum while the imaging head moves. An example of this approach is the Optronics 2000 (Figure 5-22).

In internal drum imagesetters, film is automatically fed from a roll onto a drum, then the imaging head travels along a spindle through the inside of the drum to image the film. The image head rotates as it moves along the spindle. Internal drum imagesetters include the Agfa SelectSet 5000 and the Scitex Dolev.

Figure 5-22. The Optronics 2000 imagesetter was one of the first PostScript-compatible drum-based imagesetters.

Flatbed imagesetters are low in cost and can serve a variety of needs. They are, however, generally limited to 12-inch width material and may not provide the high quality output for color separations or items where registration is required. Examples of these include the Agfa Proset 9800, Linotronic 330, and Varityper 5300.

Drum imagesetters provide a high quality and utilize blue-light laser diodes which image on blue light-sensitive film. This film can cost 30 percent less than red light-sensitive film. The disadvantage of drum imagesetters is that a full sheet of film must be exposed each time regardless of the size of the final image needed.

With the advent of desktop publishing, most of the new imagesetters are now PostScript compatible and use a raster image processor (RIP) that translates the PostScript code into the actual spots on the film. The spots are written with a laser.

Another approach to imaging other than the laser is the use of light emitting diodes (LED). The Itek LED film recorder uses a chip with 24 LEDs and lenses to focus the light to 1260 to 3200 dots per inch.

While we have been talking primarily about color separations, at least one internal drum scanner using tungsten light has been designed for exposing Ektachrome film to produce high-resolution transparencies. The Fire 1000 from Cymbolic requires 18 minutes to image a frame at 50 line pairs per millimeter using a 20 micron spot.

Still Video to Copy Printer

APPLICATION BRIEF

A government location in the midwest United States uses a 2-chip Sony ProMavica camera to capture images of printed circuit boards that have been exposed to destructive testing and prints the images four-up on an 8 1/2 by 11-inch page on a Canon Color Laser Copier 500. The still video system is also used to take and print public relations pictures and other images. The cost savings of the installation were so good that the complete system was paid for in five months.

Digital Proofing

Before the printing presses run, the printshop customer usually wants to see page proofs that will show what the pages will look like when they come off the printing press. Several different kinds of page proofs are available.

Thermal-wax printers and inexpensive color inkjet printers can provide color pages suitable for checking a concept or page design. Simply said, these concept or design proofs only give an idea of what the final image will look like. The colors are not likely to be very close to those produced on the printing press.

The next higher quality level proof is the continuous tone image generated by thermal-dye transfer printers and high-quality inkjet printers. These proofs, however, do not show the halftone screens of the printed page, and therefore cannot be used to spot problems such as moires, dot gain, and register. Contone proofs can provide a good indication of what the printed colors will look like.

Contone printers that can output digital files and PostScript files are available from companies such as Tektronix, 3M, and Agfa. These printers are suitable for proofing PostScript color pages.

Direct Digital Color Proofing

A new type of proofing device has been developed to produce halftone color proofs directly from the computer files. These direct digital color proofing (DDCP) devices provide a high-quality image automatically on the same paper that will be used by the press. For example, the DDCPs can output the halftone color images on newsprint stock for newspaper proofs or on high-quality coated paper for glossy magazine proofs.

The proofs produced by the DDCP devices are intended to

Figure 5-23. The Kodak Approval Digital Color Proofing System provides proofs directly from a color electronic prepress system. (Courtesy Eastman Kodak)

be the equivalent of the contract proofs given to ad agencies and publishers by service bureaus or printers. Some of the more widely used contract proofs are Du Pont's Cromalin, 3M's Matchprint, and Kodak's Signature. Both 3M and Kodak have come out with DDCPs. The 3M Digital Matchprint system uses a liquid electrophotographic process, while the Kodak Approval DDCP uses a dry laser process (Figure 5-23).

The digital proofs, like their photographic contract proof equivalents, reproduce the actual halftone screen that will be used on the press plates, and can include variables such as dot gain, dot shape and size, and screen angles.

Issues Affecting Color Proof Printing

In most thermal-wax printers, the paper is not held in registration, which means that there will be some slight variations in the placement of the colors from page to page. There are exceptions in more expensive printers where the paper is held in registration.

The causes of the registration problem include things such as how much moisture the paper has absorbed as well as the fact that each sheet of paper may be handled differently by the rollers of the color printer.

There is also the limit of 300 dpi resolution of thermal-wax printers. While 300 dpi is good enough for a rough proofs, presentations, and business reports, it is not good enough to serve as a printer's proof. If you give a 300-dpi color proof to a printer and he uses it as the basis for measurements, the dimensions may be 1/32 or 1/64 of an inch off.

If that weren't enough, the paper in the thermal-wax proof is probably totally different from the paper that will be used on the press. That's one of the advantages of a proof print from a high-resolution inkjet printer, such as ones made by Iris and Stork. These inkjet printers can output a proof on the paper that will be used on the press.

There is also a need for a great deal of education for people involved in the production cycle of both photography and of printing. In photography, a transparency or color print always has less than what the eye would see in the actual scene. When the photograph is converted to a halftone color image, the glossy proof will have less color values than the photograph. When the halftone image is run on a press, the color image will have less color values than the proof.

Printing customers have become used to seeing Cromalin or Matchprint glossy proofs that show 120 percent of what they get in the final printed product. In other words, the glossy proofs have a better image than what will finally print. This has led to the expectation by inexperienced customers that the printer was going to be able to deliver a higher level of quality than is actually possible. The experienced customer soon learns that the glossy proof is only a goal for the printer to try to achieve in the final printed product.

Glossy contract proofs have become a benchmark in the printing process. The proofing process is changing. There are more choices in the kind of proofs that can be used. An inkjet proof, for example, can more closely approximate the colors that will be produced on the press by using the same paper as the press. Service bureaus and printers can

Digital Imaging of Planets at Cornell

APPLICATION BRIEF

When analyzing the scientific make-up of Neptune and Jupiter, Cornell University's Dr. Reid Thompson and co-investigator, Dr. Carl Sagan, relied on an Agfa Matrix analog film recorder to output digital image data sent back from the Voyager space probe. The 35mm transparencies produced by the Matrix recorders are used for analyzing the properties of Neptune and Jupiter and their moons.

electronically modify glossy proofs to show press run effects such as dot gain. But the printing customer still has to learn how to interpret these proofs. For the service bureau and printer, that means they must continually provide a customer training program.

Direct to Press Printing

Now it is possible to take the digital photograph and any accompanying copy from a desktop publishing system directly to a printing press without going through the step of making the CYMK separation films. Presstek and Heidelberg have teamed up to develop a new digital press called the GTO-DI, which completely bypasses CYMK film output (Figure 5-24). With the GTO-DI, color bitmap files are sent directly to cylinders on the press.

Blank plates are mounted on the press cylinders. The three-layer plates have an ink-repelling silicon layer on top, aluminized conductor in the middle, and an ink-accepting mylar base. Tungsten electrodes scan slowly across the rotating plate and each burns in one raster line by means of arc-spark erosion. The resolution is 1016 dots per inch. The total make-ready time from mounting blank plates to full speed printing is about 15 to 17 minutes. Once up to speed, the Heidelberg press runs through 6000 sheet per hour. The press uses a dry offset process, which means that water is not needed in the printing process.

This new Presstek-Heidelberg system is in its early stage, but it already produces good quality color. Proofing is one of the problems that still must be overcome since there is no guarantee that a proof made on a printer or any other proofing device will match the output of the plates that are burned in on the press.

Other companies are also developing digital presses. Some claim that they will have the capability to change the

Figure 5-24. The Heidelberg GTO-DI direct-to-press system, being developed by Presstek, Inc., takes digital data from a variety of sources and sends the bitmapped page data to an arc-spark unit on the press that burns the images onto the CYMK plates. Once the four plates are imaged, the press is ready to run. (Courtesy Digital QuickColor Inc.)

imaging on every page at full press speed. If such capabilities are developed, then digital presses could revolutionize the entire printing and publishing industry.

Beauty Parlor Previews with Color Video Prints

APPLICATION BRIEF

New Image Industries uses a Sony color video printer to give beauty parlor customers a preview of how they will look with a new style, color, frosting, or perm. The New Image Salon System is a video-based system that combines computer, video, and still-image technology to bring full-color images of how a variety of haircuts and styles might look on customers. The company also makes video/computer imaging systems for landscapers, interior decorators, architects, and house painters.

Standards for Digital Photography

With all of the sophistication available today in digital and video cameras, desktop computers, color screens, and printing technologies, it would be desirable if the final output color could be checked automatically and predictably. The problem is that the colors produced by the phosphors of a computer's CRT display do not match the colors of the cyan, yellow, and magenta inks used in printing, or the dyes used in photographic materials.

Several companies are working to develop standardization tools for each of the components in the digital photography equation. The Dicomed Color Advantage system of algorithms, for instance, can be used to match color across the various components of the digital photography equation from the input device to final hard copy output.

Eastman Kodak is developing a Color Management System that takes into account the individual characteristics of each component, and uses a "precision transform" to establish a computationally efficient relationship between a device-dependent color space and a device-independent color space.

With the Kodak Color Management System, the color characteristics of a scanner and of a printer are individually characterized and a precision transform is associated with each area. Then the colors on the color display being used are characterized using a screen color calibration device. When you put these together, you can wind up with something close to the color you see is the color you get (CYSICYG).

Kodak likes to relate this approach to George Eastman's original advertising slogan, "You push the button and we do the rest," only today's version is, "You click the mouse and we do the rest."

The approach by Tektronix to the problem of color device color accuracy has been to develop sophisticated TekColor correction algorithms that resolve color performance differences between input and output devices for the Macintosh. TekColor is mainly used in Tektronix and Macintosh QuickDraw color printers.

Several different standard projects are currently being pursued both by the American National Standards Institute (ANSI) and the International Standards Organization (ISO). The Committee for Graphic Arts Technology Standardization (CGATS) is working to define color measurement standards for graphic arts applications.

The ANSI IT8 committee has developed the first generation of digital data exchange standards (DDES), which provide a common exchange format for digital files used in electronic design workstations and prepress. The IT8 standards serve as the basis for the international standards approved by the ISO. The IT8 standards allow color data to be moved from desktop and workstation design systems to prepress systems, and to transfer data among prepress systems made by different vendors. One of the standards deals with the problems of on-line transfer of digital color data between a prepress system and a direct digital color proofing (DDCP) system.

The IT8 committee also is developing standards for the color calibration of input scanners. The IT8 group also is working to create a preferred or default three-component color standard for graphic arts using RGB as opposed to the CYMK that has traditionally been used.

All of this work in standards, as well as color management, will allow better merging of all of the components of the digital photography equation.

CHAPTER 6

Multimedia Applications

The word "multimedia" has long been used as a descriptor for presentations that combine more than one way of presenting information, such as combining slides with motion pictures and sound. Later with the entry of desktop graphics software, printed text, graphs, illustrations, and video became important parts of multimedia.

Today mutimedia has acquired multiple definitions. The U.S. Olympic postage stamp set, designed by computer artist Joni Carter, has been described as a multimedia event because she used motion video of the various Olympic events to capture her initial images and then used a personal computer and paint software to create the actual stamp artwork.

Multimedia has been adopted as a promotional buzzword by many manufacturers. Whether it is a computer manufacturer who has a platform that can bring in a video signal, an audio manufacturer who has a board that can add sound to a computer, or a variety of other specialty items including color printers and image projectors, they are all part of the growing field of multimedia.

The real key to multimedia is the integration of text, graphs, illustrations, still photographs, live video, and sound in the personal computer environment (Figure 6-1). It is important to note that just bringing in the images is not enough. It is also important to be able to edit these images and make good effective use of these images and the other

Multimedia Helps Create Olympic Stamp Set

**APPLICATION
BRIEF**

Sports artist Joni Carter uses an IBM multimedia studio with two PS/2 computers. One PS/2 loaded with M-motion software is used to call up and display color video footage of athletes in action that have been stored on laser disks. The computer images replace photographs, slides, and even live models in the studio. The artist's second PS/2 is her painting computer where she sketches and paints her artwork on the screen. Thermal-dye transfer prints are used for proofs. The Olympic track and field commemorative postage stamp set was the first to be painted and printed from start to finish using a computer.

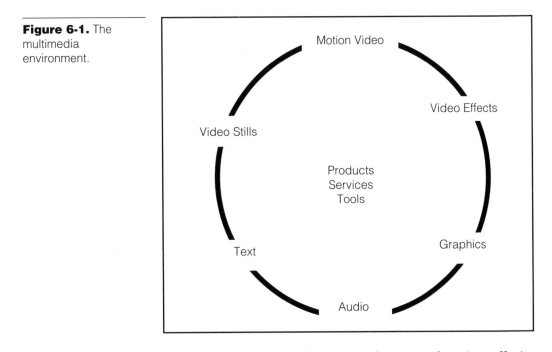

Figure 6-1. The multimedia environment.

Motion Video

Video Effects

Video Stills

Products
Services
Tools

Graphics

Text

Audio

elements of multimedia. It sounds easier than it really is, but there has been a great deal of progress. One of the problems has been the enormous amount of memory that is needed to store the color and video images used in multimedia. Being able to store all of the material at a reasonably economical cost has certainly been the challenge and goal of the major manufacturers.

The seriousness of purpose of the various manufacturers is shown by the joint venture of IBM and Apple Computer. Called Kaleida, the new organization was formed to develop technologies for multimedia.

If there is one thing that will be required from people who use multimedia, it will be restraint. It will be very tempting to use all of the elements possible to create a multimedia program. In many cases, this will be unnecessary, expensive, and may ultimately diminish the effect on the individuals who view the program.

You can't help but think of some of the initial and justified concerns when desktop publishing first arrived. The concern expressed by the those who developed some of the original desktop publishing programs was that users would "put madras jackets with plaid pants." In other words, they would forget the elements of good design. That concern is even greater with the use of multimedia. Multimedia brings tremendous power to the desktop, but its real value will be measured by how effective it is in communicating, and not in technical virtuosity.

The real importance of multimedia is the ability to create an interactive program. People learn more easily when they are part of the learning experience. Interactive multimedia programs have been created for diverse fields such as welding and surgery, and they are finding increasing use in public schools.

Multimedia, with its combination of technologies, will offer great opportunities for both the developers of hardware and software. The effect of multimedia will be felt in almost every area of business and education. Ultimately, the home may be affected to the greatest extent.

Multimedia High School Yearbook

APPLICATION BRIEF

A multimedia yearbook was produced by high school students at South Eugene, OR. Photos from the printed yearbook were scanned into a Macintosh computer, then merged with audio clips of marching bands, lecturing teachers, and cheerleaders. The electronic book was produced on a CD-ROM disk for the Macintosh II and was entitled "The Electronic Eugenean."

Software for Multimedia

The key driving force for multimedia is software. The challenge is the merging of all of the different elements considered to be multimedia into a common screen and audio-channel and doing all within the practical limitations of the computer and the storage system available.

Major companies such as IBM, Apple, and Commodore have all been working actively on multimedia for a number of years. While not all of these companies have included video images and high-quality sound, most have included text, graphics, and recently, digital photographs.

IBM software encompasses both the DOS and OS/2 operating systems. Storyboard Live, which has been available for some time, is an easy tool for creating everyday business visuals (Figure 6-2).

IBM's OS/2 Audio Visual Connection, together with new video-capture and audio adapter cards, makes it possible for both experts and non-experts to capture and edit sound and images, create special effects, and produce interactive presentations with professional quality, high resolution, and full color. Video images can be digitized for storage and later use, photographs can be digitally stored, screens can be captured, images can be enhanced, audio can be digitized and enhanced, text can be added, and story sequences can be edited.

Other programs that have been developed and have served well on the IBM platform include Animator from AutoDesk, Rio from AT&T's Graphic Laboratory, and Lumena from Time Arts.

For DOS systems running Windows 3.1, Microsoft has extensions that contain software hooks for special multimedia drivers.

Figure 6-2. The IBM PS/2 computer. (Courtesy IBM Corp.)

Figure 6-3. Apple's QuickTime user interface allows Macintosh applications to play video sequences.

With the advent of Apple's System 7, Apple has added QuickTime, a software architecture that allows developers to integrate dynamic media, such as sound, video, and animation, across all applications (Figure 6-3). The software comes with a movie toolbox and an Image Compression Manager that allows software and hardware developers to take advantage of compression schemes such as DVI, Group 3 fax, and MPEG. A component manager allows external system sources such as digitizer cards, VCRs, and system software extensions to register their capabilities with Macintosh system software so that any application can access these capabilities.

MacroMind provides a family of products for use with Macintosh computers. MacroMind Director has become almost a standard for creating interactive multimedia presentations and animation. The software provides a set of tools that allow users to create and combine text, graphics, animation, sound, and video (Figure 6-4). The software adds interactivity and control for devices such as video tape recorders, video disks, and CD-ROMs.

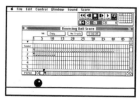

Figure 6-4. MacroMind Director uses a score window to organize the elements of an animation sequence.

Included with the Director software is the MacroMind Macintosh Player, a run-time (for program playback only) utility that allows users to distribute and play back documents created on Macintosh computers without having to run the application program.

The MacroMind MediaMaker allows the integration of video with graphics, animation, and sound to make videotapes and create video presentations.

There are a number of other software packages for multimedia. Some are specialized production tools. For example, AutoDesk Animator Pro offers a variety of animation tools for real-time 2D animation. The program has tweening (transforming one shape into another over a range of frames), optical animation (classic swirls, twirls, spins and flips), titling, color cycling (changing an object's color over a specified time), and cell animation. A full-featured paint package is included as well as an Animator ProPlayer, screen-capture utility. The software also provides links to a variety of other systems.

There also are audio and music software packages for creating high-quality sound tracks for use in multimedia products.

CNN Uses Still Image Transmission for China Coverage

APPLICATION BRIEF

Cable News Network made use of Sony's Still Image Transmission System to send photographs of the recent student uprising in China to its Atlanta headquarters. Photo courtesy Cable News Network.

Boards and Specialized Chips for Multimedia

Each of the major platforms for multimedia—Macintosh, PC, and Amiga—has its own advantages. The Apple Macintosh began as a platform that favored graphic applications, while the IBM and compatible PCs offered speed and processing power. The Commodore Amiga developed special capability for handling standard (NTSC) video signals. For each of these different platforms, hardware additions have been necessary to optimize the handling of sound, animation, and video.

The IBM M-Motion Video Adapter/A receives analog signals from external video and audio sources, processes, digitizes, and sends them to the OS/2 monitor and external speaker for immediate viewing in multimedia application solutions. Slow motion can be mixed with VGA computer graphics. The audio portion accepts music, voice, or other input, and the signal can be digitized and stored within the OS/2 computer.

Matrox has taken a different approach in their board design for DOS-based PCs. The Matrox Illuminator plugs into an ISA bus. It combines video in and extensive graphic processing in a Windows environment.

VideoLogic makes their DA-4000 board product line available in versions for DOS or OS/2 PCs and the Macintosh. The PC version allows two video signals to be displayed simultaneously. The Macintosh version includes an on-board graphics processor so that a graphics adapter is not needed.

The Media-Link board family from Spectrum Signal Processing uses a high-speed interconnect bus that manages data transfers and provides fast, efficient communication between the PC host, digital signal processing chips, and peripherals independently from the host system bus. The

Figure 6-5. The Spectrum DSP/PC Single Board Computer and the Media-Link SSP42C100 Controller Chip. (Courtesy Spectrum Signal Processing Inc.)

Spectrum system eliminates the bus bottlenecks and system constraints that have been a problem in PC systems (Figure 6-5).

The Media-Link architecture is built around a custom chip called the Media-Link Controller, which transfers data between processors at 66 megabytes per second.

Other chips are making an impact on multimedia. C-Cube's compression/decompression processing chips have grown in compression capability, and they also meets the JPEG standards for compressing digital photographs.

Digital video-compression chips are particularly important because of the huge amount of memory required to store uncompressed video images. Some of the first demonstrations of compression and reconstruction required as many as a seven chips. Single-chip devices quickly followed and provided lower-cost compression/decompression.

Boards are being developed to meet the sound needs of multimedia. The Pro AudioSpectrum board from MediaVision includes 22 simultaneous instrument sounds, professional sound mixing, an output amplifier, and stereo digital-to-analog converter. The board includes MIDI sequencer software that allows the standard MIDI sound files or music composed in the computer to be played using the MediaVision board.

Training Packaging Machine Operators

APPLICATION BRIEF

Tetra Pak is a Swedish company that manufactures machines that package liquid food products. Tetra Pak uses Sony View workstations to run their interactive training programs. These programs train machine operators working at customer plants on the proper control of Tetra Pak liquid-filling machines.

Multimedia Vendors

IBM's development efforts for multimedia began about 1980 when two researchers, one in Denver and one in Atlanta, started to experiment with an interactive system that was built with a predecessor to the first IBM PC, a video tape player, and some touch technology from an outside vendor. When the system was demonstrated to key IBM management, they were so impressed that the project was funded and work proceeded.

An internal IBM study in 1983 found that the company's education costs were about $1.2 billion per year and climbing. So in 1984 IBM established "Guided Learning Centers" with self-study systems that utilized computer-based training, text-based training, and programmed instruction.

In 1985, another development program led to the introduction of IBM InfoWindow touch-display system. By 1987, a catalog of 196 courses for InfoWindows was available. By 1990, InfoWindows courses, in a variety of disciplines, exceeded 1000.

IBM expects multimedia to become a part of the way we work, learn, and live. With integration of voice, music, still images, full motion video, film, graphics, text, and touch, the personal desktop computer will become an information appliance and a personal communicator.

In 1984, Apple Computer created the Macintosh computer, which paved the way for the integration of graphics into mainstream applications. The delivery of the Macintosh System 7 and QuickTime in 1991 provided a platform for a whole new generation of multimedia applications and extended the capability of existing applications. The new joint effort of IBM and Apple Computer promises to result in further expansion of multimedia.

The Commodore Amiga computer has long been regarded as an inexpensive alternative for video production. The success of programs like Video Toaster points out the capability of the Amiga computer in the processing and production of video images.

Other companies are also entering the multimedia platform area as well. Sony with its experience in optical disk recording, imaging video, and electronic photography, has moved these strengths into the production of equipment and software for multimedia. The Sony VBOX Controller is a computer-video interface that allows personal computer users to control a wide range of Sony consumer video peripherals, including video decks and 8mm camcorders, from their presentation and multimedia software.

Another use of the VBOX is for integrating full-motion video into multiscreen presentations. Up to seven Sony VBOX controllers can be daisy-chained and connected to a computer through a single serial port, allowing multiple video devices to be cued and controlled during a multiscreen presentation. This is similar to the original slide-and-movies multimedia presentation technique, but now it is controlled and cued from the PC.

Other companies are beginning to move into the field of multimedia. Digital Equipment Corp. sees the opportunity of supplying both workstation and networking for multimedia. JVC, with its range of imaging cameras and other peripherals, and Hitachi, with its printers, CD-ROM drives, cameras, and other peripheral equipment, are two examples of Japanese companies that have begun the move into multimedia.

Other Japanese companies such as NEC and Fujitsu are developing sophisticated chips for use in the multimedia. These chips will increase the speed of processing, quality of images, and permit more video windows to be opened at the same time in multimedia software.

Figure 6-6. A Tandy computer designed for multimedia. (Courtesy Tandy Corp.)

Tandy Corp. provides a line of fully configured multimedia personal computer systems. Available with internal or external CD-ROM drives, the systems exceed the minimum hardware requirements for multimedia PCs and have full compatibility with industry-standard software (Figure 6-6). In addition, the Tandy multimedia PCs are compatible with Kodak Photo CD, which provides a standard means for high-quality digital photograph storage.

Browsing Illuminated Manuscripts on Interactive Video

APPLICATION BRIEF

The J. Paul Getty Museum in Malibu, CA, has a valuable collection of illuminated medieval Renaissance manuscripts. Browsing by visitors would destroy the fragile pages. The solution was an interactive video system that enabled visitors to browse through the high-resolution color video images while listening to an audio tutorial on how the books were made.

Image Compression for Multimedia

The JPEG standard for digital photography compression partially solves still-image storage problem, but the compression of motion video is still a challenge that is being addressed by the Motion Picture Experts Group (MPEG).

An early motion video compression method was developed at the David Sarnoff Research Center (formerly RCA Laboratories) in Princeton, New Jersey. Called digital video interactive (DVI), this compression technology is now being marketed by Intel.

DVI is based on proprietary compression-decompression algorithms and a video-graphics chip set that carry out the decompression processing and produce a real-time video display (Figure 6-7). The two-chip DVI set consists of a pixel processor and a display processor. The pixel processor is designed to process at 12.5 million instructions per second (mips). By comparison, an IBM PC AT runs at approximately 2 mips. The display processor gives DVI its resolu-

Figure 6-7. Putting multimedia on CD-ROM disks using the Intel DVI process. (Courtesy Intel Corp.)

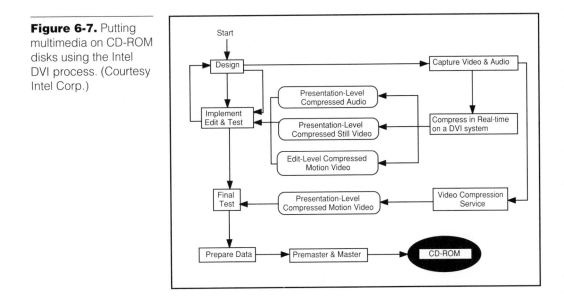

tion modes and pixel formats. Resolutions can range from 256 to 1024 pixels horizontally and up to 512 pixels vertically.

After compression, a DVI CD-ROM disk can hold one hour of full-screen, full-motion video, or up to 16 hours of 1/8-screen video at a half frame rate. By mixing video, stills, and sound, you could put, for example, 20 minutes of full-motion video, 5000 digital photographs, six hours of sound over stills, and 15,000 pages of text on one CD-ROM. Because MPEG has been slow in establishing its standards, DVI technology has moved ahead on its own.

The Video Compressor software included in Apple's QuickTime uses an image compression method developed by Apple. It is designed to permit fast decompression with good picture quality. The software can do both spatial and temporal compression. If only spatial compression is used, compression ratios of 5 to 1 to 8 to 1 produce reasonable quality. If both spatial and temporal compression are used, the ratio extends from 5 to 1 to 25 to 1.

On a Macintosh IIcx, it takes half a second to decompress a full-screen color image and about 3 seconds to compress the same image. On a Macintosh IIfx, compressing a full-screen image requires one second and decompression time is 0.2 second.

Video compression can be achieved by a completely different approach proposed by Iterated Systems. Their proprietary compression technology uses fractal-based compression algorithms. Using only software-based fractal compression and decompression, full-motion color video is possible with playback speeds up to 30 frames a second on a standard VGA PC.

The fractal approach uses mathematical descriptions or formulas. The key is a development of Dr. Michael Barnsley of Fractal Transform that completely automates fractals.

Using the transform, only a few seconds are required to find fractal formulas for very complicated still or moving pictures (Color Figure 6-8).

Another company, UVC, has produced an integrated multimedia processor with compression ratios of 20 to 1 and 30 to 1 at 30 frames per second with the capability of reaching 500 to 1. The patented UVC compression algorithm differs from JPEG-approved discrete cosine transform, and the UVC transform is claimed to be about 50 times less complex than the JPEG one. The UVC processor takes each scan line, samples the analog signal, and digitizes it using UVC algorithms. The digitized data is then compressed. In addition to video processing, the processor can accept and compress digitized 12-bit audio.

Using UVC's algorithms, Total Multimedia has built a software package called SoftVideo that can play back compressed images at 30 frames per second at VGA resolution on an AT (286) personal computer. Recording with SoftVideo requires a hardware addition to compress and record video at frame rates.

Business Presentations with Electronic Still Video

**APPLICATION
BRIEF**

Cincinnati Bell relies heavily on electronic photography equipment from Sony to lend immediacy and polish to its presentations. With ProMavica still-video cameras, Cincinnati Bell can incorporate a wide variety of video images into their presentations quickly and easily—anything from pictures of their potential customer's current facility and equipment to images of corporate executives taken when they arrive for their presentation.

Evolving Standards for Multimedia

Completion of video compression and decompression standards, as well as graphics standards and interchange standards, is necessary for the success of multimedia. The standard for digital photographs that has been developed by JPEG has won general acceptance, and the new technologies like fractal compression may become extensions to the JPEG standard. Efforts by MPEG to establish a video standard have been much slower. The ultimate standards needed for multimedia may come from the Apple-IBM joint effort, Kaleida, for the development of multimedia.

Although software and hardware developers are providing the first impetus for multimedia, its ultimate success will require that both industry-wide and international standards be developed and implemented.

Some Views of Multimedia

A phenomenon of multimedia is that its parts can be viewed as the whole by some users, according to Bill Coggshall, New Media Research Inc. Some users, for example, might see multimedia as a way to incorporate and manipulate audio using a personal computer. On the other hand, graphic artists who produce special effects will use many more of the tools that are available.

Surprisingly, experts hardly ever mention hard copy as one of the dimensions of multimedia. Paper and film output will continue to be a necessary part of multimedia production. It wasn't too long ago that an earlier generation of computer affectionados talked about the "paperless office"—a phenomena that has yet to happened.

Peter Blakney, IBM's manager of market support for multimedia, points out that his company has been offering multimedia since 1986 with their PC-based InfoWindow program for interactive video disks. While some people want to see very sophisticated programs, Blakney likes to point out how IBM is using multimedia to try to solve some fundamental problems such as illiteracy.

Apple Computer's Kirk Shorte prefers to use the term "media integration" to describe multimedia. He sees the field as a family of technologies and estimates that there is a worldwide market potential of $12-24 billion. His view is that the goal of multimedia is to add sound and video to the computer.

When you talk with Commodore people, they point to their development of the Amiga computer as a video platform. Combined with AmigaVision software, the computer offers a powerful video editing system at a low price.

A completely different approach comes from Microsoft, which has set up a multimedia project group that hopes to "put a computer on every desk and in every home." Microsoft created a trademark, which has the letters MPC with a disk icon in the middle of a rainbow-colored M and the words "Multimedia PC," that has been adopted by multimedia developers for display on products that meet certain standard multimedia specifications for PCs (Figure 6-9).

Figure 6-9.
Multimedia trademark created for display on hardware and software that meets certain industry multimedia standards. (Courtesy of Microsoft Corp.)

The specification calls for an AT (286), 10-MHz or faster processor, or any 386 or 486 processor; two megabytes or more or RAM; at least 30 megabytes of hard disk capacity; a VGA display; a digital audio subsystem; a CD-ROM drive; and compatible systems software. Microsoft is using its Windows software as the basis for multimedia applications. The Windows specification allows for alternative systems software as long as it is compatible with the Windows applications interfaces.

That means that hardware and software that carries the MPC-Mutimedia PC trademark will be compatible with the Microsoft multimedia specification. According to the developers's group, "The trademark is designed to be a symbol of plug-and-play functionality in the same way that the VHS trademark signals compatibility among video cassette players, recorders, and tapes." The original sponsors of the trademark include AT&T, CompuAdd, Creative Labs, Fujitsu, Headland Technology, Media Vision, NEC, Olivetti, Philips, Tandy, and Zenith. An industry organization is to take over ownership and licensing of the trademark.

MacroMind's director of product marketing, Dave Kleinberg, sees multimedia as "an investment in data" and feels that content is important. He believes that users will have to achieve real cost savings if multimedia is to achieve success.

An old Chinese saying aptly summarizes multimedia, according to IBM's Blakney:

If you tell me, I will listen.

If you show me, I will see.

If you let me experience it, I will learn.

These words of Lao Tse from 420 B.C. are a good summary of multimedia—what it is—what it can be.

CHAPTER 7

The Future of Digital Photography

Changes in digital photography and its related fields—digital television, still-video cameras, multimedia, personal computers, etc.—can be expected to occur steadily and rapidly. Some of the changes are predictable, others are not. In order to make predictions, one first must have some kind of perspective of the key developments that have already taken place.

Throughout the first half of the twentieth century, the movement toward electronic imaging progressed slowly. Television brought electronic images into the home, but the average person could only watch broadcasts. With the advent of video cameras and camcorders, and the video cassette player-recorder, home videos became popular. But still-video cameras, such as Sony's Mavica, did not catch on with the general public, which still prefers film cameras for still photography.

Today developments in television, personal computers, and photography are converging in ways that will create a need and a market for digital photography. High-definition television and digital television are being introduced worldwide. Personal computers now have the power to handle color images efficiently, and image processing on the computer will be the "darkroom" of tomorrow. Analog still-video and digital cameras are becoming good enough for use by professional photographers. Newspapers and newsmagazines routinely use electronic cameras to photograph fast-breaking events. Electronic imaging in photography is moving forward at an ever increasing rate.

A parallel development in the area of personal computers certainly is worth mentioning. The personal computer was introduced by Apple in 1975 and by IBM in 1981. In less than a decade, the personal computer has become irreplaceable (at least to many people) and today it is the platform of choice for digital image processing.

Magazine Digitizes Color Pages

**APPLICATION
BRIEF**

Hearst Magazine's Victoria had two reasons for doing its own digitizing of color pages—gaining time and saving money. Electronic publishing eliminates a number of costly prepress steps. More importantly, by working with color electronically, publishers now literally save days each month in production time. The power of production is placed in the hands of graphic artists and designers, who find that the computer dramatically increases the amount of creative time available.

The Global Economy

The image processing of today had its roots in the programs of the National Aeronautics and Space Administration (NASA) in the 1960s. At that time it was mainframe computers or very large minicomputers that were required for image processing. Today desktop image processing is commonplace, and portable computing and perhaps optical computing may be the systems of choice in the future.

The leadership in the development of software for digital photographic processing currently is in the United States.

The emergence of programming expertise in other parts of the world may seriously challenge the U.S. A report published by the U.S. Department of Commerce claimed that the U.S. is losing in the development of digital imaging technology versus Japan and Europe. The same report indicated that the U.S. was losing in sensor technology against Japan but holding its own against Europe. This tells us that if you are looking at digital imaging technology, you must look at all parts of the world for future developments.

The globalization that so many companies are talking about is beginning to happen to the entire area of digital photography. While some digital camera innovations have come from the U.S., more have come from Japan. Some electronic printing technologies have been developed in the U.S., while other technologies have come from both Japan and Europe.

Globalization will continue. A wider vision will be necessary to be able to take advantage of the available opportunities in the imaging marketplace.

Another sign of the globalization is the agreement by the Massachusetts Institute of Technology to export its American-style creativity to a Japanese university. The Japanese are eager to copy MIT's unique Media Laboratory, where hard-headed science blends with imagination. The MIT lab has a loose and creative atmosphere; that is rare in Japan.

We also are seeing the beginning of a significant convergence of art, photography, and electronics. Some call the results of the combination "artware," and it is expected to affect not only conventional photography and art, but also entertainment.

Even with an ordinary desktop PC or Macintosh computer and a scanner, it is possible to take a photograph and make it into something new, challenging, and creative. Tomorrow with the advent of better scanners combined with more readily available optical storage, new hard copy output devices, and most importantly, with new user-friendly software, people who never thought they had art skills will be able to create and visualize the art of the future.

Hands-On Photo Studio of the Future

APPLICATION BRIEF

Studio 2000 was designed to demonstrate to professional photographers the powerful synergies created by the marriage of film-based photography with computerized image enhancement. Staffed by a crew of computer and photographic experts, Studio 2000 featured an extensive array of state-of-the-art electronic image processing hardware and software from Kodak and other vendors.

Electronic Imaging—Where Silver Meets Silicon

Companies such as Eastman Kodak see today as a time when the silver of the photographic imaging is meeting the silicon of electronic imaging. For over 100 years, imaging has been a silver-halide-based technology. Now there is an irreversible movement toward a digital photographic environment. We have already felt the impact of electronic processing on the printing and publishing industry. More and more we see film-based photographic images are being scanned and made into a digital images. With the advent of digital cameras, the growth of digital photography will accelerate.

In printing, the traditional way in which printing plates are made, using film negatives to expose the plates for the press, is being challenged with the introduction of direct computer-to-plate systems that image the press plate without the intervening film step. The next step already under development is the digital press, with on-press imaging of the plates. Ultimately, a variable digital press will be able to be able to change the contents of the page it prints while it is running. This new technology, initially very expensive, will continue to grow and improve because the need exists for on-demand color printing and for continued high quality.

Where is digital photography going? It is one of the most difficult questions one could ask. The quality of the digital image is of primary concern. Most electronic cameras still do not produce film-quality images. Many electronic still-image cameras produce images that appear to be at the level of a video image from a camcorder.

That brings us to the difference between a film image and a video image. When you talk about a "film look," you are describing an intangible. Part of the film look is the color range in the image and the the shape of curves in the shadows and highlights. The "video look" usually means that skin tones lack tones and highlights, and the overall image lacks sharpness. Another feature of the video look is that the hair of a person lacks detail. One of the factors contributing to the video look is the nature of the color portion of the NTSC video signal and its low resolution.

Kodak has gone beyond the NTSC standard with its Photo CD and digital still-video camera. People who have seen the Photo CD product have been surprised by its film-like images, even on a video screen. In the case of the Photo CD, Kodak has gone to four times the resolution of proposed HDTV standards, while their still-video camera back has twice the operating resolution of HDTV systems.

Emerging Technologies

Advances in processing power, electronic storage, and communications have made it possible to place the digital photograph in our computers for processing, storage, and retrieval. Today's microprocessor has the power of yesterday's minicomputer; tomorrow's microprocessor will have the power today's supercomputer at a small fraction of its cost. Dr. Donald Greenberg of Cornell University sees workstations reaching the level of supercomputers by 1995 with over 100 mips of power.

Memory

Storage of digital information once was costly. Less than a dozen years ago, PCs used a 5 1/4-inch floppy disk with 100 kilobytes of capacity. Now 3.5-inch disks for PCs routinely hold 1.44 megabytes—14 times more than the 100 kilobyte disk. New high capacity 2-inch disks are being used in laptop computers and electronic camera systems. Optical storage systems with erasable capability and increasing speed of retrieval are becoming a meaningful part of digital image processing.

Memory (RAM) chips on standardized plug-in cards have become affordable and offer another means of storing digital data (Figure 7-1).

Communications

In order to be able to transfer digital photographs from one place to another, we will need high-speed communications systems. Transmitting images over existing telephone wires is possible, but we are approaching the limits of the transmitting capability of copper wire. Fiber optics holds the promise of the future, but the installation of the vast new systems will take some time.

Japan's Nippon Telephone and Telegraph (NTT) hopes to have fiber optics to every Japanese home, business, and

Figure 7-1. Random-access (RAM) memory chips are used for temporarily storing information in electronic systems. As the capacity of RAM chips has grown, the cost per megabit has dropped rapidly, as shown in this chart of prices for static RAMs. (Courtesy Yosuke Nakajima, Fuji Photo Film)

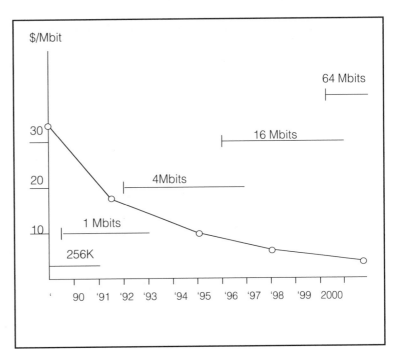

school by the year 2015. Singapore, whose telephone system was once an antiquated system, today sports a state-of-the-art network. All of this effort has been made in Singapore in order to attract investment.

However, there is hope with new developments such as the system designed by the ImageSpan Division of GTE Corporation. Their system allows text and pictures to flow over copper telephone lines and satellite at rates as high as 1.5 million bits per second. This is much faster than the current transmission speed of 2400 to 9600 bits per second.

Figure 7-2. The Sanyo still picture videophone enables a still image from the camera to be transmitted, received, and displayed on the monitor. (Courtesy Sanyo Fisher Corp.)

Videophones and video conferencing are both enjoying a resurrection (Figure 7-2). In recent years, with increased concern for the safety of their traveling personnel, companies turned to video conferencing and videophones to provide person-to-person meetings, for the relay of product information and drawings, and for the transmission of color and black-and-white photographs. Video conferencing continues to grow with the advent of new CODECs (code-decode devices for signal transmission). Standardization has been achieved for CODECs, which is expected to lead to much more usage for these devices.

While we talk about digital photography, there still looms the concern over the legal ownership of copyrights of images when several are included and merged in image enhancement systems. There is also great concern for the editorial responsibility associated with the modifications to digital photographs.

Photographs have been retouched by hand for many generations, but today it is possible not only to retouch, but also to make major alterations to the picture and to change the actual scene. A famous example of this is the cover of the February 1982 issue of *National Geographic* in which a photograph was electronically altered to move pyramids closer together.

There are a number of proposals to identify photographs that have been manipulated. While enhancement or efforts to make the picture clearer, much like the hand retouching of years ago, is deemed acceptable, it has been proposed that manipulation of the image should be identified with some designation in the actual photograph. A proposal from Norway suggests that the word "Montasje" be used, with the M given extra prominence. The hope would be that the large M would become a standard.

Object-Oriented Programming

Object-oriented programming, some say, will change the future of computer programming. Already object-oriented programs for imaging exist, even though they are not well publicized. The big advantage of object-oriented programming is that you can reuse the objects you create in different programs. This means, for example, that a program that involves enhancement can have an object move to a program that is word processing.

Macintosh computers use electronic objects called file folders and file cabinets to organize pages of information similar to the way you would create files in an office or home. This is one form of object-oriented programming.

Unix, an operating system for computers developed by Bell Laboratories, has won high acceptance among workstation manufacturers. The Open Software Foundation, a consortium of leading hardware manufacturers, including IBM, Digital Equipment, Hewlett-Packard, and others, will exchange elements of their proprietary systems in an effort to create an open version of Unix that will run across their own and other hardware platforms.

The OSF was formed when Sun Microsystems joined with AT&T to create a separate Unix standard called OpenLook. While Unix has been a very exciting development tool, only recently have efforts been made to make it a user-friendly system and one that requires very little expertise to operate.

Companies are developing new systems that will greatly affect the future of digital photography. Polaroid has for some time been working on new technologies for digital photography. Their plans and technology demonstrations have included digital still cameras, films that develop with heat, as well as an X-ray system called Helios that uses no silver and produces digital images. While most of these products still lie in the future, it still shows that Polaroid sees digital photography as a future market.

Japanese companies are equally interested in digital photography and the means of capturing digital images with CCD sensors. Fuji has not only developed a digital camera but also storage systems for digital photographs and a system for digital X-rays.

Sony, with its experience in digital VCR and video processing, can be expected to show more in the area of digital still

Figure 7-3. Sharp's 100-inch LCD projection system utilizes liquid crystal display technology and a variable zoom lens. (Courtesy Sharp Electronics Corp.)

photography in the future. Matsushita, Sanyo, Toshiba, and Konica all will play important roles in electronic imaging.

Already, manufacturers like Mitsubishi and Sharp are looking seriously at the home market for theater-like presentation centers. Sharp has developed a 100-inch LCD projection system (Figure 7-3).

Firms in Japan have not been hesitant to show their technology. To celebrate its 70th anniversary, Olympus Corp. held a technology fair that demonstrated present and future products (Figure 7-4). Most companies in Japan are working on the next generation of computer architecture, with emphasis on digital imaging.

An example of the innovative designs that have been presented in Japan is the Hitachi digital combined still and motion video recording system. With a single camera, the home video buff has the opportunity of making both still and movie images, all on 8mm video tape. The movie

Figure 7-4. A view of the Olympus Technology Fair that was staged as an exposition of present and future trends in visual communication. (Courtesy Olympus Corp.)

images can then be displayed on a home TV, while still images can be viewed on the TV screen or finished prints can be made on a color video printer.

A technology of the future that is already here is the Sharp system for sending color faxes. Called ColorFax, it can send a high-quality 8 by 10 color image in three minutes. At the receiving end, a thermal-dye transfer printer outputs the color page.

3D Imaging

Photography with three-dimensional realism has come and gone. A few people still actively pursue conventional 3D photography. More attention now is being paid to 3D computer-aided design, which enhances visualization. Three-dimensional video also is receiving attention.

The first 3D video images required glasses with colored or polarizing lenses to produce a depth effect. A more sophisticated approach followed, in which liquid-crystal shutters were synchronized to send different images to the right and left eyes. Companies such as Dimension Technology and Nippon Telephone & Telegraph have developed screens that produce 3D images without the use of special glasses.

Dimension Technology uses an LCD with light stripes that allow the viewer to see the right and left eyes without the use of glasses. The NTT system uses a lenticular system similar to that used on printed 3-dimensional postcards.

Interest in three-dimensional images has led to a new technology called virtual reality, which combines vision, sound, and hand movements to create the feeling of being able to see and touch objects that exist only in the computer.

Current virtual reality systems use a helmet with a pair of color LCDs, one for each eye, and stereo headphones (Figure 7-5). The wearer has a helmet with a sensor that tells the computer when the head moves. A special glove senses hand and finger movements, which can be used to manipulate objects in the scene being viewed.

The first virtual reality systems used rather simple graphics to depict "reality." In the future, we can expect to see realistic images in three dimensions, which will bring new excitement to the world of computer imaging. Virtual reality can be used for interactive simulations, problem solving, and perhaps even for interactive movies.

Holograms are another form of three-dimensional imaging. Polaroid has developed a method to generate holograms using a computer. Researchers in MIT's Spatial Imaging Group have demonstrated that it is possible to project 3D holographic images. Perhaps this is the first step in achieving the science fiction accounts of transmitting holographic images in real time to create life-like three-dimensional images.

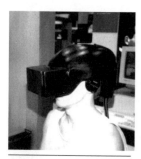

Figure 7-5. This virtual reality helmet has two LCD screens and stereo headphones that create a realistic three-dimensional effect.

Developments in Chip Technology

One of the drawbacks of current digital cameras is the lack of CCD sensors with a sufficiently high resolution to create "film-look" images. Most of the mass-produced CCD sensors have only about 380,000 pixels and the ability to record 2 to 2.5 million bits of color data.

The Kodak digital camera system has a CCD that can produce about 10 million bits of color information. You might notice that I do not refer to pixels. As the development director of a major film firm once said, trying to compare film and electronic images using pixels is like comparing apples and oranges. Each pixel in a CCD sensor is capable of creating from 1 to 14 bits of color information, depending on the dynamic range of the device and the system that is receiving the image. He noted that a silver grain in a film image is turned on only once.

What makes the Kodak digital camera system more costly than other still-video cameras is the high-resolution CCD used. These CCDs are not the mass-produced camcorder CCD sensors. Kodak produces its own high-resolution CCDs.

Experimentation continues for new techniques for creating CCD sensors. Olympus Optical has work in progress on a static induction transistor (SIT) imager that has ten times the sensitivity of conventional CCD sensors. Combining the SIT imager with an amplified solid-state imager developed by NHK, in cooperation with Olympus, has the potential for a major advancement in digital photography. The amplified solid-state imager uses field-effect transistors to eliminate noise, which is one of the problems that makes it difficult for sensors to achieve their full sensitivity and color capability.

Philips Research Labs in the Netherlands is experimenting with indium and tin-oxide solid-state sensors. By putting dense rows of indium-tin-oxide on silicon wafers, Philips hopes to produce light sensors with high sensitivity.

Memory chips for computers have rapidly grown in capacity. With memory modules, the jump was quick to 4-megabit chips, but already 16-megabit chips are being produced both at Texas Instruments and IBM.

IBM is looking at X-ray lithography to keep help with the growing density needed for new generations of chips. X-ray lithography is expected to play a part in IBM's 64-megabit memory chip expected by the mid-1990s. By the year 2000, memory chip capacities could reach as high as 1000 megabits using X-ray technology. IBM is not alone in their interest in X-ray technology, Japanese manufacturers also are working in the same direction.

Efforts are being made to speed up the basic operation of CPUs, the heart of microcomputers. The next generation of microprocessor from Intel will be the 586 microprocessor with more than 3 million transistors. This massive chip is designed with a superscalar RISC technology and will deliver performance of over 100 mips. Supercomputer performance may well be at the desktop level by the mid-1990s.

Lasers

Lasers are another technology that is becoming significantly improved. Laser manufacturing improvements have resulted in lower-cost lasers that also have lower power needs. Companies such as 3M are using lasers in printers that produce photographic-quality digital color prints.

For a number of years, predictions have been made that gallium arsenide (GaAs) would replace silicon in computer chips. Electrons move five to seven times faster through the silver-gray GaAs crystal than they do through silicon.

Figure 7-6. The Sony chip that uses artificial intelligence to control home entertainment centers. (Courtesy Sony Corporation of America)

The GaAs material, however, is brittle and has proved to be difficult to produce. Now it appears that ways of mass producing gallium arsenide have been developed. GaAs chips have promise for significantly improving many of the items needed for digital photography.

While all of this high-technology work on chips goes on, artificial intelligence may help make it easier to control and operate electronic equipment. Sony's SIRCS II (Sony Infrared Remote Control System) chip uses artificial intelligence to control living room audio and video systems (Figure 7-6). SIRCS allows component controls to make decisions on an "if-then" basis, with the result that nearly all the control functions have been reduced to simple, one-touch operations.

Neural Networks

At first look, neural network technology may seem to have little to do with digital photography. Neural network technology, which mimics the neural system of the brain, has developed to the point where it is being used for applications such as text recognition and image processing. For image enhancement, intelligent look-up tables, and many of the day-in and day-out decision-making portions of digital photography, neural networks may serve a important and helpful role.

New neural tools are appearing on a regular basis. Intel Corp. has developed a neural network chip that can learn and remember what it has been taught. The neural cells of the chip consist of two EEPROMs, solid-state memory units that can be electronically altered.

Will we see neural networks tomorrow in digital photographic systems? Possibly in cameras for some of the judgmental aspects such as exposure, contrast, and focus. Sharp has introduced a set of chips that use neural network technology to perform a broad range of image processing applications. The chips are intended to act as an interface between image-capture hardware, such as CCD cameras and scanners, and the host computer system. What is significant is that these chips imitate what occurs in human visual processes and can recognize complex objects almost instantaneously.

The Sharp Image Processing System is being sold to equipment manufacturers, along with tools that enable them to develop products based on the neural network

Figure 7-7. The Sharp neural network image processing system is sold as an application development system. (Courtesy Sharp Corp.)

technology (Figure 7-7). In a demonstration, Sharp used a video camera and frame grabber to digitize a video of a train moving on a circular track. The neural network system demonstrated that it was able to recognize the image of the train by placing a box around the train that moved along with it.

Applications of neural network technology in photography and publishing include high-speed image scanning, transmission of images over phone lines or between networked computers, and sophisticated text recognition. Other applications are machine vision for quality control in manufacturing and photographic systems that can recognize faces or certain objects.

In digital photography, neural networks in image processing systems could be used for tasks such as color correction, adjusting colors in a digitized image so it will look better on the screen and when printed. Or the system could enhance portions of a photograph that have muddy tones or other weaknesses.

Sharp is not the first company to demonstrate image

processing using a neural network system. Hecht-Nielson Corp. introduced the first PC-based neural network board for image processing in 1987. Nestor Inc. has marketed a Character Learning System for recognition of handwritten text.

Fuzzy Logic and Imaging

Fuzzy logic, invented by a professor at the University of California in Berkeley, has been adopted by a number of Japanese manufacturers. Canon and Minolta have used fuzzy logic in their still-video cameras. The fuzzy-logic chips can identify a subject anywhere in a frame. On camcorders, Sanyo uses fuzzy logic to smoothly adjust the iris, while Matsushita corrects the jiggle in hand-held camera operation with fuzzy logic. Some of the fuzzy-logic chips used in the cameras were made by U.S. companies.

Fuzzy logic mimics the reasoning of the human mind, and can deal with data using concepts such as: a few, more, or mostly. This is accomplished with "belief curves," with the top of the curve meaning that the information being received is true. Two lines with negative to positive values, which go from the top of the curve to a baseline, are used to calculate the true and false weights for a particular function.

Togai InfraLogic has created a fuzzy-logic chip that can recognize the Kanji characters in Japanese writing. Togai applied the same fuzzy logic to a single-chip device designed to classify and sort objects. The chip uses a process called differential competitive learning.

It seems obvious that combining fuzzy logic with neural networks could create a powerful means for creating "decision-making" components for all aspects of digital photography, from the camera to the processing and enhancement station, and then to the final output. Fuzzy logic and neural networks may be able to tune many of the elements of the system so that the color you see is the color you get (CYSICYG).

Optical Computing

Optical computers use light instead of electrons to process information. Although electrons travel at very high speeds, photons move at the speed of light—the fastest rate at which anything can move. That means photons can transmit data more quickly than electrons. It seems only natural that this type of computing could be used to process our photo images more easily and more quickly (Figure 7-8).

AT&T scientists have demonstrated a working digital optical processor that uses lasers to transmit information internally and employs optical devices to process the information (Figure 7- 9).

A number of universities are also working on the development of optical computers. A programmable optoelec-

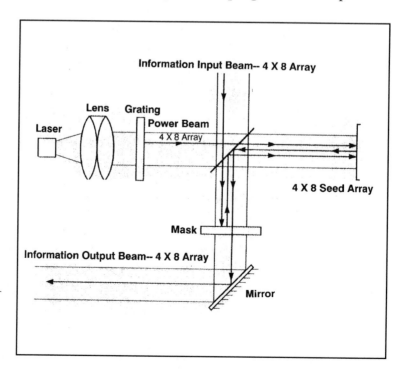

Figure 7-8. One-stage of an optical processor using an array of beams.

Figure 7-9. Bell Labs switches light beams with symmetric self-electro-optic effect devices.

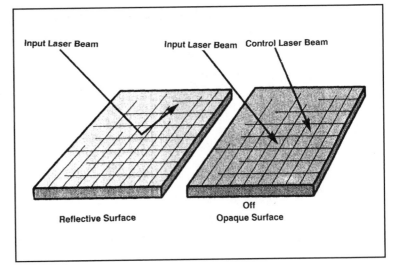

tronic multiprocessor system that uses laser light in a three-dimensional architecture to create a massively-parallel fine-grain system has been developed at University of California at San Diego. The optical computer integrates silicon processor arrays with ferroelectric light modulators.

Pieces of optical computing are being developed worldwide. Researchers at the Royal Signals and Radar Establishment in England and also the University of Grenoble in France have been able to obtain light from silicon wafers. Corning Glass in the U.S. has produced glass optical switches. Japan is looking at the potential for commercializing spatial-light modulators. Nippon Telephone's modulator can record, read out, amplify, and invert images at 2000 frames per second using ferroelectric liquid crystals.

Will the day come when an optical computer will be available for digital photograph imaging? Most experts say yes, but they point out that some critical components still have to be developed. And it is not easy to predict just when those critical inventions will be made. A veteran researcher once told me, "How do you make an invention?"

HDTV and Digital Television

Different high-definition television (HDTV) systems are under development in the United States, Japan, and Europe. The competition is intense. In the United States, there are many contending systems (Figure 7-10), but there is a high probability that a digital solution for HDTV will be selected. This will be advantageous for digital photography because the TV signal will no longer have to be converted from analog to digital and digital images will not have to be converted into analog signals.

The European standard HDTV is expected to be finalized in the mid-1990s. Japan is already broadcasting HDTV using the MUSE analog 1125 line system. This is an old technology in comparison to the new digital compression technology that is being proposed for the U.S. standard.

Figure 7-10.
Contenders for the high-definition television system that will be adopted by the U.S.

U.S. HDTV Contenders

System	# Lines	Cycles/s	Scan type
Advanced compatible television (ACTV) David Sarnoff Research Center NBC, Phillips, Sarnoff, Thomson	525	59.94	Progressive
Narrow MUSE NHK, Japan Broadcasting Corp.	1125	60	Interlaced
DigiCipher General Instrument Corp.	1050	59.94	Interlaced
Spectrum compatible HDTV Zenith Electronics Corp.	787.5	59.94	Progressive
Digital Simulcast HDTV N.A. Phillips Consumer Electronics Co.	1050	59.94	Interlaced
Channel compatible HDTV Massachusetts Institute of Technology	787.5	59.94	Progressive

Adoption of digital HDTV will create a mass market that will bring down the cost of digital cameras, camcorders, and other equipment. Competition in the HDTV marketplace will also speed up the introduction of higher resolution CCDs and other devices that will enhance the capabilities of digital photography (Figure 7-11).

Figure 7-11. Zenith's Spectrum Compatible high-definition television system screen is compared to the current NTSC standard for American television. The Zenith screen has twice the horizontal resolution and twice the vertical resolution of NTSC image. (Courtesy Zenith Electronics Corp.)

Tomorrow is Closer Than You Think

Digital photography is a reality today. The quality it can produce is approaching that of film, but some feel that it still lacks the "film look." However, as improved components are introduced, the resolution and quality of digital color images will also improve dramatically.

The era of digital photography and the digital darkroom has begun. Digital and film-based photography will continue to exist side by side for some time. Just as artists and graphic designers in the publishing field have had to learn to use the computer to create and manipulate illustrations and to layout pages, photographers will have to learn to use the computer as their darkroom to enhance, crop, and print their photographs.

Today the Macintosh, PC, and Amiga computers give you a platform to work on digitized images at reasonable cost. There is an ever-increasing array of digital photography tools to choose from. The cost of starting out in digital photography can be less than a thousand dollars; a professional digital photography studio can cost more than a hundred times that amount.

The tools that you need to get started—video and digital cameras, scanners, computers and image processing software, high-capacity memory systems for image storage, and output devices—are here and available. However, you can become overwhelmed by the technology and the changes that occur. The best way to begin is to focus on understanding the digital photograph, what it is, how it works, and what you can do with it. Begin to work with digitized images. Then you will be able to pick the right tools for your digital photography needs.

Tomorrow will bring new and amazing products for and improvements to digital photography. It's a dynamic and exciting time we live in, and we are lucky to be part of such a wonderful experience. But if you continually wait for products of tomorrow, you will not be fully participating in that experience.

Center for Creative Imaging

**APPLICATION
BRIEF**

Eastman Kodak has opened the Center for Creative Imaging in Camden, ME, as a place where people will be able to lay hands on some of the best equipment available for electronic photo enhancement.

Kodak has gathered together in the Center an array of equipment that represents the latest developments in electronic cameras, scanners, imaging workstations, film recorders, and color printers. Instruction will be provided by Kodak staff and experts from across the United States.

THE FUTURE OF DIGITAL PHOTOGRAPHY

Glossary of Terms

Algorithm. A set of rules for solution of problems, represented by sequence of stored instructions. Computer programs are an example of algorithms.

AppleTalk. A local-area network protocol developed by Apple Computer for use with the Macintosh.

Architecture. The specific components, and the way those components are interconnected, that make up a microcomputer system. Often used to describe the specific bus structure within a microcomputer.

ASCII. American Standard Code for Information Interchange. A standard coding system that assigns a numeric value to letters, numbers and symbols. The lowest common denominator for exchanging text among programs.

Aspect Ratio. The relationship between the height and width of a displayed object. A 1:1 aspect ratio means the object will appear undistorted.

Auto Trace. A feature found in some graphics programs that allows conversion of bit-mapped images into an object-oriented format. See Bit-map, Object-oriented graphics.

Bernoulli. A removable hard disk system popular in the PC-compatible. Bernoulli disks can hold 44 or 90 megabytes of data and are manufactured by Iomega Corp.

Bezier curves. A type of curve created by some object-oriented graphics programs that can be manipulated by means of endpoints and anchor points that determine its slope and length.

Binary. A numbering system employed by most computer systems that uses two numerals, 0 and 1, to represent all numbers.

Bit. The smallest unit of binary information. A bit will have a value of "1" or "0". A contracted acronym derived from Binary digIT.

Bit-Map. Images formed by patterns of dots, as opposed to object-oriented images, where shapes are formed from mathematical descriptions.

Bit-Mapped Display. A computer display that can control individual pixels, allowing the computer to show graphics in addition to text. See Character-Based Display.

Block. A unit of text or graphics that can be manipulated as a whole.

Brightness. A measure of lightness or darkness in an image.

Bus. A data pathway within a computer system.

Byte. A unit of data containing eight bits. A byte can consist of up to 256 different values. Used as a measure of file size on a computer. See Kilobyte, Megabyte.

Calibration. A process by which a scanner, monitor, or output device is adjusted to provide more accurate display and reproduction of images.

Camera-Ready Copy. Text and illustrations laid out on a page in the proper size and position, and ready to be photographed for a printing plate. See Mechanicals.

Cathode-Ray Tube. (CRT). A vacuum tube that generates and guides electrons onto a fluorescent screen to produce images, characters, or graphics.

CCD. See Charge-Coupled Device.

Central Processing Unit (CPU). The main section of a computer, which handles arithmetic and logic operations.

CGA. Short for Color Graphics Adapter, the first color display standard for PC-compatible computers. Offers limited resolution. See EGA, Hercules, VGA.

CGM. see Computer Graphics Metafile.

Character-Based Display. A computer display, commonly found in the first personal computers, that is limited to showing alphanumeric characters and simple graphic elements. Most character-based displays use a grid consisting of 25 rows and 80 columns. Each cell in the grid can contain only a single character.

Charge-Coupled Device (CCD). An image sensor used in scanners and digital cameras.

Clipboard. A temporary electronic storage area in a computer system where text or graphics can be held for reuse.

Color Correction. A process of adjusting color values to achieve the best level of accuracy for a reproduction.

Color Separation. A process by which a color page is

converted into CYMK color components. Each color can be used to create a piece of film, which is burned onto a plate or written directly to a printing press. See CYMK.

Color Separations. A set of four transparencies for making plates in four-color printing.

Comp. See Comprehensive.

Comprehensive. A page, produced during the design process, that provides a preview of how the final print job will look.

Computer Graphics Metafile (CGM). A file format used for storing computer graphics.

Continuous Tone. A photograph or illustration containing an infinite range of colors or gray shades.

Contrast. A measure of the difference among various colors or gray levels in an image. A high-contrast image shows a large difference between light and dark shades. A low-contrast image shows less difference between light and dark shades.

CP/M. An early operating system for microcomputers developed by Digital Research Inc.

CPU. See Central Processing Unit.

Crop Marks. Small marks on a page that indicate the area to be printed.

Crop. To cut or trim an illustration or other graphic element.

CRT. See Cathode-Ray Tube.

CYMK. Cyan, Yellow, Magenta, Black. These four colors

are used by printers to reproduce color images.

Data Compression. An operation that reduces the memory space required to store image data.

Default. A specification that takes effect in the absence of other instructions. Most scanner programs have default settings for variables like brightness and contrast that apply unless the user requests something else.

Densitometer. A device used to measure the intensity of gray shades or colors in a printed image. Often used to calibrate an imagesetter, scanner, or monitor for more accurate display and reproduction of images.

Desktop Publishing. The use of a personal computer to produce camera-ready page layouts for books, newsletters, magazines, and other printed material. Also refers to programs that produce page layouts. See Page-Layout Program.

Dialog Box. A pop-up window in a program that allows the user to choose among different options.

Diffusion. A filtering effect performed on gray-scale or color images that randomly distributes gray levels in small areas of an image to achieve a mezzotint effect.

Digital Halftone. A halftone produced by a computer system. See Halftone.

Digitize. To convert information to the digital format usable by a computer. What scanners and digitizers do.

Digitizer. A device that converts video signals into a digital format that can be displayed on a computer. Also used to refer to certain computer drawing devices.

Disk Operating System (DOS). An operating system for

IBM-compatible personal computers that controls basic computer operations, such as the transfer of data to and from a disk drive. Requires use of English-like commands to perform operations. Also known as MS-DOS and PC-DOS.

Dithering. A process by which an input or output device simulates shades of gray in an image by grouping dots into clusters known as halftone cells. See Halftone cell.

DOS. See Disk Operating System.

Dot. The smallest unit that can be printed, scanned, or displayed on a monitor. Dots produced on a laser printer are sometimes called spots.

Dots Per Inch (DPI). A unit that describes the resolution of an output device or monitor.

DPI. See Dots Per Inch.

Driver. A software program that controls a specific hardware device such as a frame grabber board, scanner, or printer.

Drum Imagesetter. An imagesetter in which the output media is mounted on a rotating drum.

Drum Scanner. A scanner in which reflective or transmissive media are mounted on a rotating drum.

Dye Sublimation. A color printing technology used in continuous-tone printers.

Edge Enhancement. An operation that accentuates the edge details of an image.

EGA. Short for Enhanced Graphics Adapter, a color display standard in the PC-compatible environment. Offers better resolution and color display than CGA, but is surpassed by VGA. See CGA, Hercules, VGA.

Encapsulated PostScript (EPS). A file format that stores images in the form of PostScript language commands.

EPS. See Encapsulated PostScript File.

Equalization. A process by which the range of gray or color shades in an image is expanded to make the image more attractive.

Facsimile. A technology that allows transmission of images over telephone lines by use of facsimile machines or PC fax boards.

Filter. A software function that modifies an image by altering the gray or color values of certain pixels.

FinePrint. A printing technology developed by Apple Computer that improves the resolution of text produced on a laser printer. See PhotoGrade, Resolution Enhancement Technology, TurboRes.

Flatbed scanner. A scanner, resembling a small photocopier, in which the image to be scanned is placed on a glass platen.

Font. All letters, numbers, and symbols in one size and typeface. Helvetica Bold Italic is a typeface. 12-point Helvetica bold italic is a font. Font is sometimes used interchangeably with typeface.

Four-color printing. A process that allows a printing press to reproduce most colors by mixing the three primary colors (cyan, yellow, magenta) and black.

Frame Buffer. Memory used to store an array of graphic or pictorial image data. Each element of the array corresponds to one or more pixels in a video display or one or more dots on a laser printer or other output device.

Frame-Grabber Board. An image processing board that samples, digitizes, stores and processes video signals. Typically, a frame grabber board will plug into one expansion slot within a microcomputer.

Frame. A block positioned on a page into which the user can place text or graphics.

Galley. In typesetting terminology, a reproduction of a column of type, usually printed on a long paper sheet.

Gamma Correction. A process by which the user adjusts the midtone contrast and brightness of an image.

Gamma Curve Editor. A function found in many imaging programs that allows the user to perform gamma correction operations on a color or gray-scale image. Also known as a Gray Map Editor.

GEM. Short for Graphics Environment Manager, a graphical operating environment used by many publishing and graphics programs. Developed by Digital Research, Inc.

Graphical User Interface (GUI). A computer interface, such as the Macintosh system or Microsoft Windows, characterized by the use of a bit-mapped display and graphical icons that represent common computer functions.

Gray Scale Value. A number with a range between 0 and 256 that represents the brightness level of an individual pixel in a gray scale image document.

Gray Scale. A measure of the number of gray levels in an image. Also used to describe the ability to display multiple levels of gray.

GUI. See Graphical User Interface.

Hand Scanner. A small scanner that requires the user to manually move the unit over the image to be scanned.

Halftone cell. A halftone dot created on a laser printer or imagesetter. The cell is created by grouping printer dots into a grid. The more dots present in the grid, the larger the cell appears.

Halftone. A type of photograph that can be reproduced by a printing press. A halftone breaks a continuous-tone photo into tiny dots, which the press can reconstruct with ink. The eye interprets the dots as tones and shades. The density of the dot pattern, called a screen, determines the ultimate quality of the printed reproduction. A halftone can be a positive or a negative. See Screen.

Hardware. Mechanical, magnetic, electronic, and electrical devices that make up computer. Physical equipment that makes up a computer system.

Hercules. A monochrome graphics display standard used in the PC-compatible environment. See CGA, EGA, VGA.

Histogram. A graph showing the distribution of gray or color levels within an image. The horizontal coordinate is the pixel value. The vertical coordinate shows the number of pixels in the image that use the value. Histograms give a good indication of image contrast and brightness dynamic range.

Horizontal Resolution. The number of pixels contained in a single horizontal scanning line.

Illustration Program. A program used to create object-oriented graphics. See Object-Oriented Graphics.

Imagesetter. A high-resolution output device, descended from the phototypesetter, that produces output on film or photographic paper at resolutions of 1000 dots per inch or more. Usually employs a page description language like PostScript.

Inkjet Printer. A nonimpact printer that uses droplets of ink. As a printhead moves across surface of paper, it shoots a stream of tiny, electrostatically-charged ink drops at the page, placing them to form characters.

Interpolation. A mathematical technique used in some scanning and graphics programs that can be used to increase the apparent resolution of an image. Computers usually store images as numbers that represent the intensity of the image at discrete points. Interpolation generates values for points in between these discrete points by looking at the surrounding intensities.

Joint Photographic Experts Group (JPEG). An international standard for compression and decompression of photographic images.

JPEG. See Joint Photographic Experts Group.

Kerning. The reduction of space between characters to make them fit more tightly.

Kilobyte. A measurement unit used to describe the size of computer files. A kilobyte is equivalent to 1024 bytes or characters of information.

Landscape. Horizontal orientation of pages or screen displays. See Portrait.

Laser Printer. A non-impact output device that fuses

toner to paper to create near-typeset quality text and graphics. The basic technology is similar to that of a photocopier.

Layout. The arrangement of a page, especially the spacing and position of text and graphics. Often used to describe a rough sketch.

LCD. See Liquid-Crystal Display.

LED. See Light-Emitting Diode.

Ligatures. Two or more letters that touch to form a single unit when placed next to each other.

Light-Emitting Diode (LED). A form of display lighting employed on many different office, reprographic, and consumer products.

Line Art. A drawing that contains no grays or middle tones. Even when cross-hatching and other techniques are used to simulate shading, line art is made up exclusively of black (lines) and white (paper). In Ventura Publisher, line art refers to object-oriented graphics.

Line Screen. A measure of the screen frequency, or resolution, of a halftone. Most printed halftones have line screens ranging from 65 lines per inch to 150 lines per inch.

Linotronic. The brand name for imagesetters manufactured by Linotype-Hell, including the Linotronic 330 and Linotronic 630.

Liquid-Crystal Display (LCD). LCD screens are made up of liquid crystals sandwiched between two glass plates. They are typically small and flat, and require very little power for operation.

Lithography. See Offset printing.

Local-Area Network. A system that connects microcomputers to one another, allowing them to share data and output devices.

Lossless. An image-compression function in which image data is not lost every time the compression is performed.

Lossy. An image-compression function in which image data is lost every time the compression is performed.

LPI. Abbreviation for lines per inch. Used to measure halftone resolution.

MacPaint. A paint program developed for the Macintosh computer and sold by Claris Corp. Also refers to the 72-dpi image format supported by MacPaint and many other programs.

Mail-Merge. A function, found in most word processing programs, that allows the user to create personalized form letters.

Mechanicals. Camera-ready pages on artboards or flats, with text and art in position. See Camera-ready copy.

Megabyte. A measurement unit used to describe the size of computer files. A megabyte is equivalent to 1024 kilobytes, or 1,048,576 characters of information.

Microprocessor. A single chip or integrated circuit containing an entire central processing unit for a personal computer or computer-based device.

Microsoft Windows. A software application developed by MicroSoft that manages data displayed on the CRT screen in rectangular areas known as windows. The user interacts with the software by selecting icons and menu items from the screen.

Modem. A device that allows computers to send and receive information over phone lines.

Moire Pattern. An undesirable grid-like pattern in a digital halftone resulting from the superimposition of dot-screens at wrong screen angles. Usually occurs when a halftone has been rescanned or if a dithered image has been scaled.

Monospaced font. A type style with an equal amount of space allotted for each character. Most typewriters produce monospaced characters.

Mouse. A small, hand-held device for positioning the cursor on the screen. When the mouse is rolled across the surface of the desk, the cursor moves a corresponding distance on the screen.

MS-DOS. A disk operating system used widely with personal computers and developed by MicroSoft Corp.

MSP. The graphics format used by Microsoft Windows Paint.

Multiple Masters. A font rendering technology developed by Adobe Systems that can reproduce the characteristics of almost any typeface.

National Television Standards Committee. The committee that developed the analog video signal standard—NTSC—used by the broadcast television industry in North America.

NTSC. see National Television Standards Committee.

Object-Oriented Graphics. Graphic images created by means of mathematical descriptions. They can usually be displayed or printed at the full resolution of the monitor or output device, offering more precision than bit-mapped images.

OCR. See Optical Character Recognition.

Offset Printing. A widely used printing process in which a page is reproduced photographically on a metal plate attached to a revolving cylinder. Ink is transferred from the plate to a rubber blanket from which it is transferred to paper.

Omnifont. A capability found in some OCR programs that allows them to recognize almost any font without pre-training.

Operating System. Master programs that keep all of computer components working together, including application programs.

Optical Character Recognition. The process by which text on paper is scanned and converted into text files in a computer.

Optical Disk. A form of data storage in which a laser records data on a disk that can be read with a lower-power laser pickup. There are three types of optical disks: Read Only (RO), Write-Once Read Many (WORM), and two types of erasable: Thermo Magneto Optical (TMO) and Phase Change (PC).

Orphan. A short line of text that appears at the top of a column. Many designers consider orphans to be undesirable, and some page-makeup programs can automatically remove them. See Widow.

OS/2. An operating system for microcomputers developed by Microsoft and IBM.

Overlay. A sheet laid on top of a page for spot-color printing.

Page Description Language. A programming language, such as PostScript, that gives precise instructions for how a page should look to an output device. See PostScript.

Page-Layout Program. A computer program that allows the user to create page layouts for newsletters, newspapers, magazines, and other printed materials. Also known as desktop publishing or page layout programs.

Paint Program. A program used to create bit-mapped graphics. See Bit-map.

Palette. The set of all colors available for screen displays.

Panning. Moving a graphic image inside a frame to see its various sections.

Pantone Matching System. A popular system for specifying spot colors. Each color has its own Pantone number by which it can be selected. See Spot color.

PC-compatible. A computer system compatible with the IBM-PC and its descendants.

PCX. A graphic file format produced by PC Paintbrush. Supported by many scanners and publishing programs.

PhotoGrade. A printing technology developed by Apple Computer that improves the quality of halftones produced on a laser printer. See FinePrint, Resolution Enhancement Technology, TurboRes.

Pica. A printing measurement unit used to specify line lengths, margins, columns, gutters, and so on. Equivalent to 12 points, or about 1/6 of an inch.

PICT. An image format used by many Macintosh graphics programs. Originally designed for object-oriented graphics, but can display bit-mapped images as well.

Pixel. A picture element, or the smallest addressable component of a displayable image. Used to describe resolution.

Plate. A thin, flexible sheet of metal, paper, or plastic used in offset printing. It contains a photographic reproduction of the page.

Point Size. The vertical measurement of type, equivalent to the distance between the highest ascender and lowest descender.

Point. A unit of measurement used in printing and typography that is roughly equivalent to 1/72 of an inch.

Portrait. Vertical orientation of a page or display. See Landscape.

Position stat. A photocopy or other reproduction of a halftone that is pasted onto a mechanical to show the printer how to crop and position the final image.

Posterization. A photographic effect in which the number of gray levels in an image is reduced to achieve a poster-like effect.

PostScript. A page description language developed by Adobe Systems Inc. and used by many laser printers and phototypesetters. See Page description language.

PostScript Clone. A page description language that emulates PostScript. In theory, a PostScript clone printer can produce any page that a true PostScript printer can produce.

Print Spooler. A program that temporarily stores a file to be printed until the output device is available.

Process Camera. A camera used in graphic arts to photograph mechanicals and create printing plates.

Process Colors. The four colors needed for four-color printing: yellow, magenta, cyan, and black. See Four-color printing.

Proof. A trial copy of a page or publication used to check accuracy. Also short for proofread, meaning to check for mistakes.

Protocol. A formal set of conventions governing format of data and control of information exchange between two communication devices.

QuickDraw. The portion of the Apple Macintosh operating system that handles screen display and other graphics functions.

RAM. See Random Access Memory.

Random Access Memory (RAM). Computer memory that can be read and changed. Data can be written to a particular location without having to sequence through previous locations. RAM is volatile, so all data is lost on power down.

Raster Graphics. Pictures sent to printer as bit maps (each element of picture is dot defined as black or white).

Raster-Image Processor (RIP). A piece of hardware that electronically prepares a page created on a computer system for output on an imagesetter or other device.

Read Only Memory (ROM). Computer memory containing fixed data that cannot be changed once programmed. Programming is accomplished during the manufacturing process.

Reflective Media. Print media, such as paper, that show images by reflecting light back to the eye.

Register Marks. Marks used to permit exact alignment of pages. Usually printed just outside the live area and then trimmed off. The standard register mark is a small circle with a cross inside.

Register. Precise alignment of printing plates or negatives.

Resolution. The density of dots or pixels on a page or display, usually measured in dots per inch. The higher the resolution, the smoother the appearance of text or graphics.

Resolution Enhancement Technology. A printing technology developed by Hewlett-Packard that improves the resolution of text produced on a laser printer. See FinePrint, PhotoGrade, TurboRes.

RGB. An abbreviation for Red, Green and Blue, the primary colors used in CRT display devices.

ROM. See Read Only Memory.

Sans Serif. Typestyles without little strokes known as serifs, such as Helvetica and Avant Garde. Sometimes called block or gothic.

Scalable Fonts. Fonts that can be scaled to any size from a single set of masters without loss of quality.

Scale. To change the size of a piece of artwork.

Scanner. A digitizing device that converts a piece of artwork into an electronic bit-map that can be loaded and manipulated by a software program. A means of converting hand-drawn art or photos into electronic form.

Screen. The pattern of dots used to make a halftone or tint. Halftone screens are measured in lines, equivalent to dots per inch. Tint screens are measured in percentages, with a 10-percent screen being very light and a 100-percent screen being totally black.

Screen Fonts. Digital typefaces used for screen display.

SCSI. See Small Computer Systems Interface.

Search-and-Replace. A function, found in word processors and desktop publishing programs, that allows the user to search for a certain string of characters and replace it with a another string of characters.

Separations. Transparencies or pages used for color reproduction. Each separation is used to reproduce a particular color. See Process color, four-color printing.

Serif. A tiny decorative stroke in character designs. Serif typefaces, such as Times or Palatino, use serifs in their designs. See Sans serif.

Sharpen. A filtering effect that enhances contrast around edges in an image.

Slide Scanner. An image scanner capable of scanning 35mm slides.

Small Computer Systems Interface (SCSI). An interface for connecting disks and other peripheral devices to computer systems. SCSI is defined by an American National Standards Institute (ANSI) standard and is widely used throughout the computer industry.

Soften. A filtering effect that decreases contrast in an image.

Solarization. A photographic effect achieved when a negative is briefly exposed to light. Some areas of the image are under-exposed, while others are over-exposed.

Spell-Check. A function found in word processors and desktop publishing programs that identifies and corrects misspelled words.

Spot Color. The use of one or more extra colors on a page, used to highlight specified page elements. Colors are usually specified as PMS codes. See Pantone Matching System.

Strip. To paste one piece of film, usually a halftone, into another piece of film containing a page. The film is then converted into a printing plate.

SyQuest. A removable hard disk system popular on the Macintosh. SyQuest disks can hold 44 or 90 megabytes of data and are manufactured by several vendors.

Tagged Image File Format (TIFF). A graphics file format used to store color and gray-scale images.

Thermal Transfer. A technology used in many color printers in which ink or dye is transferred to the page using a heat process.

386. A computer system that uses the 80386 microprocessor from Intel.

Thumbnail. A rough layout of a page, usually used for planning purposes.

TIFF. See Tagged Image File Format.

Transmissive Media. Film-based media, such as 35 mm slides or transparencies, that require backlighting to be seen.

Transparency Scanner. An image scanner capable of scanning transparencies.

TrueType. A typeface format developed by Apple Computer.

TurboRes. A printing technology developed by LaserMaster Corp. that improves the resolution of text produced on a laser printer. See FinePrint, PhotoGrade, Resolution Enhancement Technology.

Type 1. A format for storing digital typefaces developed by Adobe Systems. The most popular typeface format for PostScript printers.

Typeface Family. A set of all the different variations: wide, narrow, italic, bold, bold italic, of a given type design. Helvetica is a type family. See Font.

Typeface. A particular type design. See Font, Typeface Family.

UCR. See Undercolor Removal.

Undercolor Removal (UCR). A process that increased the quality of color reproduction by changing the balance of inking. The amount of ink used to print yellow, magenta, and cyan is decreased, while black is increased to produce a stronger image.

Unix. A general-purpose, multiuser, interactive operating system originally developed by AT&T Bell Laboratories.

Unsharp Masking Enhancement. An operation that produces a sharpened version of an image.

VGA. Short for Video Graphics Array, a popular color display standard in the PC-compatible environment. See CGA, EGA, Hercules.

Virtual Memory. A hardware and software mechanism in which a hard disk is used as an extension of RAM.

Widow. A short line of text that appears at the bottom of a paragraph or column. Many designers consider widows to be undesirable, and some page-makeup programs can automatically remove them. See Orphan.

Word Processor. A program used to enter, edit, and manipulate text.

Workstation. A full-featured desktop or deskside computer typically dedicated to a single person's use.

WYSIWYG. An acronym for What You See Is What You Get, meaning that text and graphics on a screen correspond closely to final printed output. Pronounced wizzy-wig.

Zoom. To view an enlarged (zoom in) or reduced (zoom out) portion of a page on screen.

List of Manufacturers

Adobe Systems Inc.
1585 Charleston Rd.
Mountain View, CA 94039-7900
415-961-4400

Agfa Division Miles Inc.
200 Ballardvale Street
Wilmington, MA 01887
508-658-5600

Aldus Corp.
411 First Avenue South
Seattle, WA 98104-2871
206-628-2320

Apple Computer Inc.
20525 Mariani
Cupertino, CA 95014
408-996-1010

Barneyscan Corp.
1125 Atlantic Ave.
Alameda, CA 94501
415-521-3388

Canon U.S.A. Inc.
One Canon Plaza
Lake Success, NY 11042
516-488-6700

Commodore Business Machines Inc.
1200 Wilson Dr.
West Chester, PA 19380
215-431-9100

Corel Systems Corp.
1600 Carling, Corel Building
Ottawa, Ontario Canada K1Z7M4
613-728-8200

Dicomed Corp.
1200 Portland Ave.
Minneapolis, MN 55440
612-885-3000

Du Pont Imaging Systems
65 Harristown Rd.
Glen Rock, NJ 07452
201-447-5800

Eastman Kodak Co.
Rochester, NY 14650
800-242-2424

Epson America Inc.
20770 Madrona Ave.
Torrance, CA 90503
310-539-9140

Fractal Design Corp.
510 Lighthouse, #5
Pacific Grove, CA 93950
408-655-8800

Fuji Photo Film U.S.A. Inc.
555 Taxter Road
Elmsford, NY 10523
800-FILM-FUJI

Fujitsu America Inc.
3055 Orchard Drive
San Jose, CA 95134
408-432-1300

Hewlett Packard
16399 West Bernardo Drive
San Diego, CA 92127
619-487-4100

Hitachi Denshi America Ltd.
150 Crossways Park Drive
Woodbury, NY 11797
516-921-7200

Hitachi Sales Corp. of America
401 W. Artesia Boulevard
Compton, CA 90220
213-605-2537

Howtek Inc.
21 Park Avenue
Hudson, NH 03051
603-882-5200

IBM Corp.
1133 Westchester Ave.
White Plains, NY 10604
800-431-2670

Ilford Imaging Systems
West 70 Century Rd.
Paramus, NJ 07653
201-265-6000

Image-In, Inc.
406 E. 79th St.
Minneapolis, MN 55420
612-888-3632

Iomega Corp.
1821 West 4000
South Roy, UT 84067
801-778-1000

Iris Graphics, Inc.
6 Crosby Dr.
Bedford, MA 01730
617-275-8777

JVC
41 Slater Drive
Elmwood Park, NJ 07407
201-794-3900

Kyocera Electronics Inc.
100 Randolph Road
Somerset, NJ 08875
908-560-3400

Linotype-Hell Co.
425 Oser Avenue
Hauppauge, NY 11788
516-434-2000

Macromind, Inc.
410 Townsend St., #408
San Francisco, CA
415-442-0200

Management Graphics, Inc.
1401 E. 79th St.
Minneapolis, MN 55425
612-854-1220

Matrox Electronic Systems, Ltd.
1055 St. Regis Blvd.
Dorval, Quebec Canada H9P2P4
514-685-2630

Microsoft Corp.
One Microsoft Way
Redmond, WA 98052
206-882-8080

NEC Technologies
1255 Michael Drive
Wood Dale, IL 60191
708-860-9500

Nikon Inc.
1300 Walt Whitman Road
Melville, NY 11747
516-547-4200

Oce USA, Inc.
5450 N. Cumberland Ave.
Chicago, IL 60656
800-342-1766

Optronics, Div. of Integraph Corp.
7 Stuart Rd.
Chelmsford, MA 01824
508-256-4511

Panasonic Industrial Co.
One Panasonic Way
Secaucus, NJ 07094
201-348-7620

Pantone Inc.
55 Knickerbocker Rd.
Moonachie, NJ 07074
201-935-5500

Polaroid Corp.
549 Technology Square
Cambridge, MA 02139
617-577-2000

Quark Inc.
300 South Jackson
Denver, CO 80209
800-356-9363

Radius Inc.
1710 Fortune Dr.
San Jose, CA 95131
408-434-1010

RasterOps
2500 Walsh Avenue
Santa Clara, CA 95051
408-562-4200

Ricoh Corp.
155 Passaic Avenue
Fairfield, NJ 07006
201-882-2000

Scitex America Corp.
8 Oak Park Drive
Bedford, MA 01730
617-275-5150

Screen USA
5110 Tollview Drive
Rolling Meadows, IL 60008
708-870-1960

Sharp Electronics Corp.
Sharp Plaza
Mahwah, NJ 07430
201-529-8200

Sony Corporation of America
Sony Drive
Park Ridge, NJ 07656
201-930-1000

Stork Bedford B.V.
35 Wiggins Ave.
Bedford, MA 01730
617-275-9446

Sun Microsystems, Inc.
2550 Garcia Ave.
Mountain View, CA 94043
415-960-1300

Tektronix Inc.
26600 SW Parkway
Wilsonville, OR 97070
503-685-2675

Texas Instruments Inc.
13500 North Central Expressway
Dallas, TX 75265
214-995-2011

3M
3M Center Building
St. Paul, MN 55114-1000
612-736-0801

Toshiba Video Systems
82 Totowa Road
Wayne, NJ 07470
201-628-8000

Ventura Software Inc.
15175 Innovation Drive
San Diego, CA 92128
800-822-8221

Xerox Corp.
Xerox Square
Rochester, NY 14644
716-423-5090

ZSoft Corp.
450 Franklin Rd. Suite 100
Marietta, CA 30067
404-428-0008

INDEX

A

Analog still video   24–30
Analog-to-digital conversion   32
ANSI   132
Applications
  broadcasting   29
  industrial   27
  multimedia   135–152

B

Black-and-white images   97
Boards
  accelerators   54
  compression   72
  for motion   142
  for multimedia   142
  graphics   55–59
Broadcasting   31

C

Calibration
  of displays   107
Camcorders   7, 23
CCDs
  as replacement for image tubes   18
  color   21, 36, 165
  description   19–23
  in scanners   8, 37
  new technologies   165
  resolution limitation   25
CD I systems   49
CD-ROM   12, 46
  drives   146
Charge-coupled devices. *See* CCDs
Charge-injection devices. *See* CIDs
CIDs   22
Color fax   163
Color look-up tables   56
Color separations
  by imagesetters   125–133
  from DTP programs   77
Color standards   14
Color trapping   81
ColorStudio   64
Commodore Amiga   145, 151
Compression   44
  chips   33, 143
  for multimedia   147
Copiers
  color   13, 118

D

Copyrights
  for photos   160
CRTs. *See* Displays
CYMK colors
  in printers   113
  separations   78

DATs   45
Desktop publishing software   76–82
Digital photograph equation   4–7
Digital signal processors   58
Digitizing   32
  analog signals   1
Direct-to-press printing   130
Discrete cosine transform   71
Disk drives
  as storage devices   12
Displays
  color   15
  CRT monitors   106
  LED   106
  plasma   111
  soft proofing   105
  used in digital photography   11
  VGA   56
Drum imagesetters   125
Drum scanners   39
Duotones   97
DVI   147
Dye sublimation printers   114
Dynamic range
  of sensor   23
  of video camera   97

E

Electroluminescent panels   112
EPSF format   84
Ethics
  of photo manipulation   160

F

Fiber optics   158
Film recorders   13, 123–124
Film scanners   41
Filters
  in LCD displays   110
  used with CCDs   22
Flat screens   110
Flatbed scanners   39

W

Windows
  image-editing programs   64
  multimedia support   139
  software packages   10
Workstations
  in digital photography   66
WORM drives
  archival applications   45
  as storage medium   12
Write-once optical disks. *See* WORM drives

X

Xapshot   26, 30